Down the Aisle

For the Love of Horses

Leslie McDonald

Copyright © 2010 Leslie McDonald with Whitehall Publishing. ISBN 13: 9781478200963. All rights reserved.

For more information contact:

Down the Aisle Promotions
5555 St. Rt. 132
Batavia, OH 45103
contact@DowntheAisleStories.com

Cover Photography by:
Doug Froh

Cover Design by:
Ascender Graphix
http://ascendergraphix.com/

This book may not be reproduced in whole or in part in any form or by any means, electronic or mechanical, including photocopying, recording, or by any information storage and retrieval system now known or hereafter invented, without written permission from the publisher, Whitehall Publishing or from Leslie McDonald.

Magazines, E-zines and other journalists are welcome to use excerpts from the book in their articles and stories. We ask that you include our website for contact purposes:
http://DowntheAisleStories.com.

Printed in the United States of America.
Retail Price: $19.95

Dedication

This book is dedicated to all the special souls
who have graced my aisle
with their love, hope and promise
that have so enriched my journey.

And, especially to Doug,
who shares not only my life,
but my dreams and passion for all the
wonderful horses down my aisle.

Endorsement

Leslie McDonald is not only a well respected horsewoman who is insightful enough to apply the lessons learned from each teacher (equine or human) as she continued her journey *down the aisle*, but she is also a woman who has *"been there, done that."* From trying to figure out how to juggle marriage and a career, live up to the expectations of those around you, survive a divorce and business setbacks along with some serious injuries, Leslie has shared her true experiences with her readers in this book.

While you are reading **Down the Aisle**, you will see yourself in the pages and realize that someone else really does understand who you are! Bonnie Marlewski-Probert, creator of the **Horse Tales for the Soul** books, http://horsetalesforthesoul.com.

Table of Contents

Introduction 6

Chapter One, *Jambalaya* 9

Chapter Two, *The Little Red Bus* 15

Chapter Three, *Tic-Tac* 25

Chapter Four, *Flo's Sanctuary* 38

Chapter Five, *Spellbinder* 50

Chapter Six, *Beneath the Ivy* 64

Chapter Seven, *Crimson Rust* 78

Chapter Eight, *On the Road Again* 90

Chapter Nine, *The School Marm* 101

Chapter Ten, *Full Cry Farm* 110

Chapter Eleven, *Murphy's Law* 119

Chapter Twelve, *The Warmblood Revolution* 134

Chapter Thirteen, *The Mighty Quin* 150

Chapter Fourteen, *My Memorable Mentor* 168

Chapter Fifteen, *Magnificent Garage Sale* 184

Chapter Sixteen, *Shared Horizons* 197

Chapter Seventeen, *Czarina of all Equine* 205

Chapter Eighteen, *Making Magic* 214

Chapter Nineteen, *Vintage Defined* 228

Epilogue 242

Down the Aisle
Introduction

Fifty years of walking forward down the aisle. Boot heels scuffing concrete, brick, limestone, whatever the composition that would lead to my ultimate destination. Those steps were my brightest source of childhood anticipation and adult fulfillment. Infected with a healthy dose of horse fever, it didn't mellow with age as my lifetime addiction passed well beyond desire into insatiable passion.

Senses were activated by the first whiff of pine shavings and the fragrance of fresh-cut timothy hay that wafted out the Kentucky doors to draw me in from the stable yard. Each stall window cast shafts of sunbeams through the bars to streak the aisle with morning light, reflecting the munching, snorting, stomping breakfast harmonies that resonated off the varnished walls.

Down the aisle each stall housed a unique occupant who had shaped my character, inspired imagination and directed the phases of my life from childhood to adolescence to maturity. They offered proud, broad backs that had carried me and my dreams through the years as student, trainer, instructor and friend. Chestnut, black, grey and bay, inviting faces marked by an assortment of stars, snips, and blazes. All special companions who had never failed to anticipate my arrival with individually distinctive greetings from the highest pitched whinny to the basest nicker.

Down the Aisle

Down the aisle following in the footsteps of the mentors who had inspired my steps. Those who had nurtured the first sprig of interest in the outstretched arms of a toddler reaching for a plush red horse with button eyes under the Christmas tree to the full bloom of passion hurtling off a cross-country bank to a powerful extension across the diagonal of a dressage ring. Grooming, mucking, braiding, training, teaching, whatever it took throughout the years just to maintain the opportunity to hold my place in the aisle.

The Captains, the Majors, the Colonels, the Flo's, the Dennys, the Lindas, the Michaels, all of those who had imparted their wisdom in my eye, my feel, my expression that eagerly absorbed the benefit of their years and their own personal passion. From German cavalry to Cadre Noir to former Olympians to seat-of-the-pants intuitiveness, all their influences were stirred into my bottomless stewpot of inspiration.

Echoes resonate down the aisle … a joyous child's giggle tickled for the first time by muzzle whiskers snuffling for a carrot treat; squeals of delight at being handed the reins, my very own reins attached to my very own horse for the very first time; whoops of elation at airing a four-foot triple bar with room to spare; breath caught in awe at the marvelous sensation of the controlled power of piaffe; soft tears choked in the throat at the passing of an irreplaceable companion; and, all the quiet spaces in-between, filled by the chirp of English barn sparrows and the muffled

Down the Aisle

mealtime munching of teeth scrapping the bottom of corner feeders in search of the remaining scraps of oats.

Take a walk down my aisle that stretches through the years past faces, both equine and human, who have shaped a horsewoman's contours and made the passage so rich and memorable. Come … walk forward down the aisle with me.

The first hint of horse fever appeared Saturday mornings riding Champion the Wonder Horse with Roy Rogers and Dale Evans at the Double B Bar Ranch.

Down the Aisle

Chapter One
Jambalaya

In the summer of 1954, Dad introduced me to horses. It wasn't because he had a personal fondness for them. In fact, I never once saw him ride. But, he must have wanted to feed the early blossom of my passion. It was most evident to all our family and friends in the worn fur of Ginger, the stuffed Palomino who was always clutched in my right hand no matter what the occasion. Twice my mother had replaced my companion's threadbare mane with scraps of white yarn from her knitting basket. Linus and his blanket had nothing over me and my Ginger.

All the signs of horse fever were present even at that early age. The Howdy Doody toy box in the corner of my bedroom overflowed with stuffed horses of every shape, color and fabric. The seat of my Dr. Denton pajamas was nearly worn through from countless hours rocking on Champion, the red wooden Wonder Horse who was permanently stabled at the foot of my bed. Saturday morning television was reserved for the adventures of Roy and Dale riding Trigger and Buttermilk at the Double R Bar Ranch.

Down the Aisle

Three months before my fourth birthday, Dad noticed a farm sign on the outskirts of Park Ridge advertising fresh produce and pony rides. Long before the pastures were paved over with subdivisions and supermarkets, and the main runway of Chicago's O'Hare International airport was expanded to within a quarter mile of our house there was open country just minutes from our front door.

On weekends a steady stream of "city" parents, children in hand, lined up along the white-washed wood corral at Richardson's Farm. There, four chunky Shetland ponies led by four chunky Richardson teenagers, would shuffle each child around a worn dirt oval for five minutes.

The speed never varied. The course never changed. But, it didn't matter to the tiny hands that clutched the worn leather reins or curled tight into the fuzzy manes. They were no longer mounted on the nickel-a-ride rock-and-roller plastic horse at the local A & P grocery store. No, they were riding and breathing a real, live pony that for the next five minutes was theirs alone.

When Dad wasn't traveling on business, Richardson's Farm became a Sunday afternoon indulgence for his only child. Garbed in my official Dale Evans cowgirl hat with matching green fringed vest, and armed with a pocketful of chopped carrots, Dad would lift me into the passenger seat of his blue Buick Roadmaster. We would only talk horse as we drove the three miles to Richardson's Farm to join the line of other pony patrons.

Down the Aisle

My favorite mount was Jambalaya, a gentle chestnut pinto with a white rump that encircled his long, red tail like a bull's eye. He was my first ride and my first love. Throughout our sessions, he would emit little pony sneezes, prompting Dad to nickname him "The Pony with Hay Fever". Well, I had hay fever too, so what could be a better match? Even at that young age, I recognized destiny.

All the stirrups on the Richardson's western saddles were permanently set at one of two lengths to save time changing them to suit individual riders. If a rider's feet did not reach one of the predetermined lengths, the parent was asked to walk alongside to steady their child's leg in case of loss of balance. The freedom days of shaggy Hop-a-long Cassidy chaps and surrogate Triggers had not yet been diminished by the threat of liability suits for any barn related bump or bruise.

While the handler held Jambalaya in place, Dad's big arms would sweep me high into the air and set me lightly in the saddle, taking care that my chubby legs did not hit the pony's rump. Before we moved off, Dad would reach deep in his pants pocket and pull out a closed fist that he would hold over my head. Slowly, very slowly, he would open his hand and wiggle his fingers over my long, brown ponytail.

It was our very solemn ritual. "This is magic malfus ralfus dust, Les," he would say. "It's only given to the very best riders. With this dust, you can master the biggest and fastest horses."

Down the Aisle

Every ride, every time, there was the showering of the dust. I checked out the other children, but I didn't notice any of them receiving malfus ralfus dust from the pockets of their parents. It made me realize from those first rides that I must indeed be a very special rider if I had been singled out by Dad to receive the dust.

The dusting ritual complete, the Richardson girl would cluck for Jambalaya to shuffle off beside her. Dad would always remain at my side throughout the ride. Once I reminded him that he didn't need to stay with me because even though I couldn't reach the stirrups, I had the dust to keep me safe.

"Oh, I know you don't need any help, my independent little cowgirl," he would laugh with a squeeze to my thigh. "But, I just want to stay close to admire how well you ride. It's special for me. Okay?"

From my first ride on Jambalaya, I believed that horses could talk. There was no doubting the evidence. As we lapped the dirt oval I was certain that pony spoke, really spoke to me. He knew things about me that only my parents and grandparents knew.

Little pony sneeze then clear as could be he would say in his gravely pony voice, "Hey, Les, I'm so glad you picked me. I can see you're the best rider here, so you were smart to pick the best pony. Must be those Wheaties you had for breakfast."

Talk about magic dust! But neither the Richardson girl nor Dad seemed to hear him. The girl kept plodding along at the

Down the Aisle

pony's head while Dad walked along at my side with his hand on my leg, looking away whenever Jambalaya spoke.

In that special pony voice, Jambalaya talked about how happy he was at the farm, about the tasty carrot treats I brought him, but mostly about how much he loved it when I came to ride him.

All the way home I would chatter about what the pony had told me. Dad would shake his head in amazement. "Wow, I don't know any other little girl who can talk to ponies. That really is a special gift. But then, you do have the malfus ralfus dust. I knew it was powerful stuff, but this is amazing."

It wasn't until I was five that I made the connection that Jambalaya really spoke to me in a muffled version of my father's voice. During one of my rides while Jambalaya was chattering away about the farm sheltie that was playing beside the arena fence, he stumbled. Not hard enough to fall, but hard enough to startle Dad into grabbing my leg and waist to balance me as the pony's knees hit the ground.

"I've got you, Les. Don't worry," he exclaimed, hugging me securely until the pony regained his footing. But, it had all happened so suddenly that Dad had forgotten to change back to his natural tone from the gravelly pony voice.

He quickly looked away once Jambalaya rebalanced and found his footing. "Sorry, Les," the pony stammered apologetically between sneezes. "Don't know what tripped me up there. I'm the

Down the Aisle

most sure-footed pony on the farm. But, I knew you'd be okay because you're such a good rider."

But, it was too late. In that moment, I discovered the truth. I don't know if Dad or I was more disappointed that his secret had been exposed. On the drive home we never mentioned it, both of us pretending it hadn't happened. But after that day, Jambalaya never spoke aloud again in any of our riding sessions.

However, my disappointment didn't last for long because by that time Jambalaya and I had begun to move beyond the spoken word to communicate on a much higher plain. We had learned to talk through a lingering touch on the neck or a long, deep farewell connection of the eyes before the next child was catapulted onto the saddle by a waiting parent.

I was certain that those full brown pony eyes that looked out at me from beneath the thick forelock knew exactly what I was thinking as clearly as I knew what he felt. His voice really was there if I just took the time to listen. It was more real than Dad's gravelly voice or the magic of the malfus ralfus dust. And, now that I had heard it, truly heard it, I knew my life would always be filled with the voices of horses.

Down the Aisle

Chapter Two
The Little Red Bus

In the mid-1950's, a pint-sized little red bus began winding its route through the Chicago Northshore suburbs two times per day, five days a week plus four additional trips on Saturday. Greeted by Billie, the jovial stable groom turned bus driver, young girls and boys clamored aboard at designated stops. Clutching black velvet hard hats, the students settled into the cocoon of twelve double seats to talk horse all the way to the stable. It was definitely a no blue jeans zone as even the boots worn for the weekly lessons were polished to a high sheen.

The little red bus offered Northshore families the convenience of free shuttle service to the stable. It was just one of the many brilliant marketing bricks upon which the foundation of this amazing and unique training facility called The Academy had been built. The equestrian school begun by the Captain in 1952 had quickly became a sold-out hit with a waiting list for those who wanted to attend the cloistered environment that had been designed to fan the horse fever that burned in youngsters and adults alike.

Down the Aisle

My first ride on the little red bus occurred in the spring of 1959 when I claimed a bribe made to me by my parents. Our family had been living in Bay Village, Ohio, for four years when Dad's company transferred him back to Chicago. I was devastated by the thought of being separated from Lori, my best friend since first grade. We had shared everything from hamsters to Betsy Wetsy dolls to gum.

In an attempt to mollify my distress, Dad had promised to enroll me in riding lessons as soon as we were settled in our new home. Bribery seemed the only acceptable solution for my horse crazy heart which had not had direct equine access since the Jambalaya pony ride days. And so, my separation anxiety from Lori was placated by the promise of a weekly seat on the little red bus.

The bus route culminated with a turn down a tree-lined gravel drive that led to a large brick stable housing 80 horses. There were two long aisles of 40 horses each, one for the riding school and one for the boarders. All the horses resided in spacious walnut, tongue-in-groove box stalls. Attached to the end of the stable was a huge indoor arena, partitioned by sawhorses into two full-size sections during busy lesson periods.

A professional image was maintained throughout all aspects of the business from equestrian to equine. All of the mounts in the school string glistened from the elbow grease that was a prerequisite of every student enrolled in classes. Even the well-

Down the Aisle

used tack was constantly cleaned and oiled to nurture and extend its serviceability. All the immaculate presentation skills that the students learned had been deeply ingrained in the Captain since his childhood.

He had been the first son of a prosperous third generation Prussian horse breeder. As a young man he had followed tradition and his peers into the cavalry. But, the War forever altered many long established lifestyles including the Captain's as the devastation ravaged his homestead along with countless others.

Left without his birthright, at the armistice the Captain fled his homeland with only his wife, two suitcases and a vast knowledge of horses. His final destination was the United States where he hoped to market his equine expertise into a lucrative career that would be the financial salvation for himself as well as for family members still in Europe who lacked the means or desire to follow his escape route.

The Academy was the realization of a refugee dream the Captain had carried close to his heart across the long miles that had ultimately led him to Chicago. There, his distinguished accent, continental military demeanor and innate communication skills with horses had attracted the clientele necessary to launch his dream. His success was incentive driven to fulfill the legacy he had been forced to abandon in Europe. In short order, his business savvy gave fellow area professionals cause to regard him as the master marketer of the Northshore.

Down the Aisle

Even as his success and personal worth grew, like many World War veterans, Captain never lost sight of the struggles and depravation he had endured to rebuild his life. He and his wife continued to live modestly in a two-story brick home at the far end of the jump ring. The unremarkable structure was shaded in the front yard by a thinning elm tree. A large vegetable garden filled the entire backyard.

The garden was his wife's sole focus in her new homeland. Never a horse enthusiast, in pre-war Prussia she had fallen in love with the Captain and the gentrified lifestyle she aspired to lead after their marriage. Physical interaction with horses had never played a role in her attraction to the man or her anticipated future.

While his wife had grudgingly settled into a world that existed outside the perimeter of The Academy, the Captain submerged himself in the business. He maintained total control of the activities within his sphere, overseeing all with a vigilant eye. There was no room or tolerance for slackers or "stable bums" as the Captain decreed. Everyone on the grounds was required to have a functional purpose be it grooming horses, taking lessons or cleaning stalls which made the stable run with efficient precision.

Down the Aisle

***Always the proper gentleman, the Captain ruled
all aspects of The Academy with continental discipline.***

The teaching staff was a very closed community. In addition to the Captain, there were two full-time instructors. Lieutenant Milo, his right hand man, was also a World War refugee and an Old World compatriot with a similar deep family background in dressage. Ted Shively, third in command, was an eager young man in his early twenties who had apprenticed under the Captain since The Academy's opening. A neighborhood kid who had started mucking stalls in exchange for lessons, he had worked his way up through the system. Drawn to Ted's determination and natural affinity with horses, the Captain had

Down the Aisle

personally taken over his instruction to mold him into a New World cavalry protégé.

From June to August, the teaching ranks swelled to accommodate an increase in students enrolled in Summer Camp. Three high school age advanced level students were promoted to the rank of instructor for the flat classes. Selection for the summer jobs was a much coveted Holy Grail for many up and coming Academy riders. With the exception of Lieutenant Milo, all instructors were products of the Captain's personal military equestrian foundation. Everyone taught under his strict guidance. No outside opinions were expressed or tolerated. The Academy was not at any time a democracy.

All classes through the jumping level were conducted in very strict military style. At the beginning of lessons, students would lead their horses into the ring and line up side by side until directed by the instructor to mount. Basic directions were given cavalry style, with the command proceeded by the word "Prepare" and concluded by the word "Ho". As the riders waited to mount, the instructor would direct, "Prepare to mount". When the students turned to face the saddles, the instructor would continue, "Mount, ho." As one, the class would climb aboard their assigned mounts whether rank beginners struggling up the side or experienced jump riders smoothly swinging a leg over the saddle.

The lessons would proceed in head-to-tail fashion along the rail with the class following the instructor's commands in

Down the Aisle

unison. When the result was well-oiled precision, the Captain would nod quietly and clasp his hands behind his back. However, when chaos broke down discipline, he would pace and slap his riding crop against his boot until the distraught instructor could restore order.

Some outsiders without full knowledge of "the system" considered it restrictive and autocratic. However, for Academy students ingrained in the Captain's system, the reward was a high level of competency and a clear pathway to the understanding of Classical horsemanship. We believed totally in the Captain and worked our hardest to earn his confidence.

The Captain maintained personal responsibility for assigning specific horses to the students each week. Despite the growing lesson base, he prided himself in staying current with each rider's strengths and weakness and his ability to match them with the appropriate mount. It was rare the Captain would let a student ride the same horse on a regular basis. He believed his responsibility was to turn out well-rounded equestrians who could master a variety of horses, not just one-horse wonders with limited skills. However, despite the Captain's attempts to encourage diversity, most of us formed quick attachments to a specific four-legged partner whenever we shared a first-time memorable experience.

My first ride since the days of Jambalaya was dear, sweet Co-Co who never veered from the rail or the instructor's

Down the Aisle

commands despite my unsteady balance. With progress came my second love, Hula Girl. We shared the thrill of my first canter; a little bolder than I had dared to imagine that still left me eager for the follow-up lesson. Then beautiful White Cloud stole my heart. With him I experienced the sensation of flight, soaring easily over a two foot cross rail that seemed at least five foot as I caught my breath on that first takeoff. Co-Co, Hula Girl and Cloud were all in their own time favorites I connived to ride as frequently as possible notwithstanding the Captain's strict system of diversity.

I was bitten by the show bug after my first competition at The Academy riding dependable Co-Co to fourth place in Walk – Trot equitation.

Down the Aisle

Despite the Captain's aura of discipline, he had a wry sense of humor that appeared at unexpected times. From my first lesson at The Academy, he was unable to pronounce my last name which was Baird. The best his Prussian accent could muster was Bird. Thus, from day one, whenever he addressed my parents, it was Mr. and Mrs. Bird.

In the late 1950's, the Captain was captivated by a Commonwealth Edison television ad campaign that featured a comical singing light bulb that looked like a bird. In my case, he took my mispronounced surname and his fascination with the electric ad one step farther. Whenever I requested a favorite horse, the Captain would challenge me to sing the entire commercial jingle in front of the class if I was to have any hope of being assigned the desired horse.

At that time, I was a very shy, chunky nine-year-old who found the thought of public a capella vocalization almost unbearable. However, the incentive to ride a beloved horse ultimately overruled self-consciousness to do what was necessary to attain the ride of my heart's desire for the next hour.

Taking a deep breath and maintaining eye contact with the Captain, I would begin my off-key rendition. "Electricity costs more today you know than it did twenty-five years ago, a little birdie told me so." At the last note, the Captain would erupt into a deep, rich belly laugh and finish the song with me, "Tweet, tweet, little bird," giving me a wink and a little tweak in the ribs.

Down the Aisle

From that original solo, my first and only nickname was born. The Captain deemed it so, and thus the name stuck even with my parents. For the next eight years of my tenure at The Academy, I was known to all as "Birdie".

Ultimately, there came a day when it was time to move on from The Academy to expand my equine experience in a new direction. While the nickname stayed behind, all the lessons of horsemanship and equitation that had been deeply woven within my fabric would be carried forward to future horses and students I would one day influence.

Down the Aisle

Chapter Three
Tic-Tac

Every six months the students at The Academy anticipated the arrival of a road-worn, red Chevy pick-up pulling an aged steel stock trailer. The drivers were an odd pair. Tall Jerry with the slow drawl and silent Mike whose few words seemed to be an octave too high for his chubby frame, were very proficient at their trade.

Jerry and Mike's relationship with the Captain had been a well-forged, lucrative arrangement long before I became a student at The Academy. Each appearance of the horse traders guaranteed a stock trailer filled to capacity with green broke horses of varying sizes and colors, ranging in age from four to six years. The school horse replacements were primarily English-type Thoroughbreds or Quarter Horse crosses with an occasional fancy pony suitable for smaller students.

The exact origin of the new school prospects was a highly guarded secret. All that was ever revealed was that the horses came from "out west". Try as we might, it was impossible to trick the Captain or the two dealers into revealing the actual location

Down the Aisle

of "out west" which could mean as close as the outlying suburbs of Chicago or as far as the vast plains of Oklahoma. The secret origin only served to increase the mystery and add to the fable that developed around each arrival. Consequently, the scope of each new horse's history was only limited by the imagination of the students who gradually created personal background stories.

The acquisition of the horses and their subsequent inclusion into the school string was truly a master plan developed by the master marketer for maximum cost efficiency. The horses were purchased with minimal training from Jerry and Mike at discounted prices. Advanced Academy students waited in line for the privilege of putting the first miles on the greenies. Because their early training was done under the watchful supervision of the Captain, the sometimes death defying early rides were considered lessons. Thus, the student "trainers" paid the regular lesson fee for the privilege of often hanging on by the seat of their pants or sometimes not.

Under the student trainers, the new arrivals gained mileage from flat work to jumping. As soon as the Captain considered them safe, the horses were rolled into the school string where they started out under the guidance of older, seasoned riders. As their equine sensibility kicked into gear and the rough edges smoothed out, they gradually trickled down through the system, becoming accessible to Intermediate and potentially even Beginner classes if their temperament was amenable.

Down the Aisle

Inevitably, a child would fall in love with a tosseled forelock, dependable security over the outside course or a welcoming nicker at her approaching footsteps. If the parents were as charmed as their child, eventually the now established school horse was purchased to become the newest privately owned, paying boarder at The Academy. As the new "family member" moved from the school string to a stall in the boarders' barn, the cycle would repeat with the next arrival of the stock trailer from "out west".

With few exceptions, the majority of the 40 stalls dedicated to boarders were filled with clients and horses who had originated in the school string. Nurtured and trained up the levels under the Captain's guidance, clients rarely considered bucking the system to shop for a new horse off the grounds. In the Captain's proven opinion, The Academy offered an unlimited pool of well-schooled, sound prospects to fulfill the desire of any student wishing to purchase a horse.

In addition to the acquisition of an exclusive mount, the purchase of an Academy horse came with the added benefit of a personalized saddle rack and bridle hook. These were located in the private tack room dedicated to boarders only. If that was not enough of a tantalizing perk, new horse owners were upgraded from school string status to membership in the "elite" classes for boarders taught personally by the Captain. Access to this desired tier was gained by the simple action of a doting parent writing a

Down the Aisle

purchase check. Their signature on the bottom line transformed the adored blue-collar lesson horse from an "out west" refugee to a revered privately owned companion identified by a brass stall nameplate that informed all the world of his change in status.

Three years of weekly lessons and consistent attendance at summer camp had proudly earned me the classification of Novice Jump Rider. The three levels of jump classes– Novice, Intermediate and Advanced – had access to a whole new tier of school horses that were far more challenging than the walk, trot, canter assortment that dependably babysat the flat riders through the basics of equitation.

At 13, I was on the cusp of feeling too old to continue to sing for my mount of choice. However, my time at The Academy had not diminished the Captain's enthusiasm for a hearty chorus of the Commonwealth Edison theme song even though it had long since been replaced on television by a new ad campaign jingle. My slightly off-key rendition still elicited a hearty chuckle from him followed by the traditional "Little Bird" tweak in the ribs.

But, there was one horse at The Academy who inspired me to sing my heart out in the hope of being partnered with him. Tic-Tac was a seven year old, dark bay gelding with a white star between his eyes and a snip on his nose. He had two short hind socks that accented his springy gaits that were a favorite of many Academy students. After two years in the school string he was

Down the Aisle

steady and safe to the fences, rarely missing a stride despite the fumblings of many of his neophyte passengers.

Without admitting to being fickle, in my three years at The Academy, I had previously had three serious equine love affairs. Co-Co, Hula Girl, and Cloud had in their own time touched my heart and carried me safely up the equitation ladder, adding a new piece to my education with each new relationship. But, none of my previous favorites rivaled the affection I felt for the perky little bay gelding. With Tic-Tac, I was certain that I had finally found the "One".

From our first ride, we just seemed to click. At 15.3 hands, he perfectly fit my 5'4" frame. Riding Tic-Tac, I felt that no exercise or fence was insurmountable. His patience and rhythmic gaits helped me to finally see the stride to a fence even when confronted by the trickiest combinations. Atop my friend, I discovered the balance to master the Captain's intricate grid exercises that required me to drop my stirrups, release the reins and hold my arms out to the side like wings over eight progressive bounces. Even in the puissance jump-off at the end of Summer Camp, I was not afraid to attempt the ever-increasing heights and spread of the triple bar as long as I faced it aboard brave Tic-Tac.

Unfortunately, due to the qualities that endeared Tic-Tac to me, he had developed quite a fan club among other Academy students who shared a similar attachment. That fact was clearly evident whenever the Captain held sign-ups for one of The

Down the Aisle

Academy schooling shows that were the semi-annual highlight of the lesson program.

The shows offered equitation classes on the flat and over fences with a smattering of jumper and hunter classes for variety. The events were executed with the same attention to detail as a sanctioned competition. The fences were gaily festooned with seasonal flowers and brush. A Northshore food service catered tasty lunches and snacks designed to appeal to the palate of non-horsy parents. Students competed for the honor of winning one of the fat rosettes to sixth place with the top prize a blue ribbon hooked on the rim of a coveted silver plate cup bearing The Academy logo.

Two weeks before the show the Captain assigned the school horses to the students for the competition. While the flat classes were limited to one rider per horse, in some of the equitation classes over fences a favored mount might make 2-3 trips around the same course, packing a different rider each time.

Demand for the most popular horses frequently resembled an Oklahoma land rush. The competition between students to ride a favored horse often developed into a true rivalry that went beyond "rock, paper, scissors" to threats of riding crops at 20 paces behind the manure pile.

The 1964 Valentine's Day show marked the culmination of a six month full court press that I had been conducting to convince my parents of the absolute necessity to buy Tic-Tac. I

Down the Aisle

was signed up to compete him in the 2'6" novice equitation over fences class. My plan was to prove my acquired skills with a blue ribbon win so my parents would acknowledge the logic and necessity of my arguments.

Previously, I had tried every tactic known to a 13-year-old who was desperately in love with a horse. I had reasoned, begged and rationalized that Tic-Tac and I were fated to be together. I had assured my parents that owning a horse would improve my grades because it would make me more responsible. I had also reminded them that my two best riding buddies had recently gotten new horses and now rode in the classes dedicated to boarders for which I was ineligible due to my non-horse ownership status. My final declaration was that it would be on their conscience if some other desiring student bought Tic-Tac resulting in my certain and immediate death from a broken heart.

Much to my chagrin, all my arguments had seemed to fall on deaf parental ears. They had patiently explained that taking the big step from weekly riding lessons to the actual purchase of a horse with all the attached responsibilities and expenses was just too great a stretch for the family budget. They were also worried that the all-consuming demands of horse ownership would limit my opportunities to experiment and grow in other social and intellectual areas. Also high on their list of concerns were the increasing study demands and pressures of entering high school the following fall.

Down the Aisle

My master plan was growing desperate. I knew I needed to make them come to their senses soon before my favorite horse fell sway to the current barn rumors and was sold out from under me. I had recently heard through the grapevine that a Thursday night jump class rider had been bragging that it was just a matter of time until her parents wrote the purchase check that would move Tic-Tac to the boarders' aisle with a brass stall plate bearing her name on the owner's line. I could only hope they would hold off until after the show so I could convince my parents of my greater merit with a Valentine's Day blue ribbon win.

After countless hours of planning every detail, the implementation of my strategy should have been easy. The jump course of brightly painted poles and brush boxes was a straight forward inside-outside-outside-inside pattern that I had ridden to perfection many times in class. Even my new riding habit fit the image of my plan. I was proudly attired in canary breeches topped by a black and blue hounds tooth hunt jacket that my mother had purchased just for this show. We had made a special girls' day outing downtown to Marshall Field's English saddlery department to find the perfect habit.

As my class time approached, Mom and Dad found a prime spot on the rail among the other expectant parents. They waved as I walked down to the end of the big arena that had been cordoned off for warm-up. I responded to Dad's wave with a confident thumbs up.

Down the Aisle

"Just wait," I thought. "Just wait."

I wasn't Tic-Tac's first rider of the show. He was waiting patiently for me in the warm-up ring next to the girl who had just ridden him in a flat class. His neat braids made him look like a serious version of the cuddly companion with the unkept mane who was my heart's desire. I climbed aboard, adjusted my stirrups and trotted two practice fences under the supervisory eye of Lieutenant Milo. And, then it was our turn.

"Next on course is number 117," the loudspeaker blared, directing the spectators' eyes toward the in-gate.

For months I had anticipated all scenarios. There would be no surprises. Every eventuality had been orchestrated in my imagination. Everything except the anxiety that overwhelmed me as I trotted Tic-Tac into the ring. For no explainable reason, my nerves began to destabilize the underpinnings of my best laid plan as I kicked Tic-Tac toward the first fence, a simple brush box topped by a green and white stripped pole.

My plan was to begin the course with a bold leap, setting the stage for the rest of a daring round. In my eagerness to wow the judge and my parents with my jumping prowess, I made a big, forward move with my body that off-balanced Tic-Tac, thrusting him onto his forehand. Too far from the fence to respond to my take-off signal, he struggled to chip in an extra stride. With both of us floundering for balance, he slammed both knees into the pole, sending it flying out in front. He had to twist sideways

Down the Aisle

upon landing to avoid stepping on it as we cantered on toward the second fence.

Disaster! Balance lost from the first missed fence, I didn't have time to regain my stride to the second. We chipped in again, resulting in another dropped rail and both my stirrups.

Catastrophe! Panic mode set in as my brain scrambled to cope with the unexpected debacle. However, the harder I tried to refocus, the more the performance disintegrated. And, in less than 45 seconds, the course that had seemed to last an eternity was over. Months of planning and dreaming were dropped with the same dull thud of the jump poles hitting the ground.

I could barely hold back the tears as I returned Tic-Tac to the warm-up ring, delivering him into the hands of the next student waiting to pilot him around the course. There was only time for a quick apologetic rub of his soft muzzle before the girl was up and turning him away with bright hope in her eyes, leaving me alone and unhorsed in the busy schooling ring.

My parents were waiting for me in the barn aisle. "It's okay, Les," my mother comforted with a soft smile. "It's not the end of the world to knock down a few poles. You did a brave job."

Dad fumbled deep in his coat pocket. "Hey, wait a minute," he exclaimed. "I knew something was missing. You were in such a hurry to show off that great little horse that you forgot to take something very important into the ring."

Down the Aisle

He carefully withdrew a closed fist from his pocket and gently held it over my head, slowly opening his fingers. "The malfus Ralfus dust. I was keeping it for you in my pocket all the time. But you were so busy, I guess you just didn't remember to get it from me before you rode."

I looked at him in amazement. I thought he had forgotten our special routine that had bonded us and Jambalaya so many years ago at Richardson's Farm. As I had grown older, he had grown more absent due to the demands of his traveling job. Our private adventures together had become fewer and farther apart until most of our little shared secrets had faded into childhood memories. I started to cry again.

He let his hand slide down my shoulder to hug me snuggly against his big frame. "You did just fine, Les. I know you were trying hard today to impress Mom and me with all you've learned. Maybe the problem was you tried a little too hard.

"You need to remember the ribbons aren't the most important thing," he continued. "Besides, after a little time, they're just dust catchers hanging on a wall. The real prize is the relationship you've developed with Tic-Tac. No ribbon will ever change that. I can see he's a very special horse. No wonder you love him so much."

He nodded to my mother who reached into her purse and pulled out a flat package wrapped in white tissue and tied with a big blue bow. She squeezed my hands as she closed my fingers

Down the Aisle

around the package. "There are lots of ways to earn a blue ribbon. No matter what the judge says, you're first place with us all the way."

"Your mother and I have been planning to give you this little gift for quite a while," Dad continued. "But today seems like the best time to share it with you. We hope you'll enjoy it for years to come."

My parents exchanged silly grins which seemed highly inappropriate considering my recent embarrassing circumstances. However, for the moment curiosity overrode my disappointment as I carefully untied the blue ribbon from the unexpected gift. Pulling back the white tissue, the shine of brass caught my eye as a bright new stall plate was revealed:

TIC-TAC
Owner: Leslie Baird

"Congratulations, Les," my parents chorused. "You'll always be a winner with us. Now, let's go find that special horse and welcome him to the family with this bag of carrots."

Down the Aisle

My best buddy, Tic-Tac

Down the Aisle

Chapter Four
Flo's Sanctuary

In the 1940's, Florence Fromm could have stepped classically from the pages of Harper's Bazaar, comfortably clad in a brown tweed hacking jacket unbuttoned informally over buff-colored whipcord breeches. It would have been the norm to find her in the stable, leaning casually against a stall front housing a Gainsboroughesque Thoroughbred.

In her youth, Flo had been a tri-color champion in the hunter show ring as well as an avid first flight fox hunter until polio struck her down in 1952. Without warning, the crippling disease debilitated her legs and robbed her of the ability to ever again effectively sit astride a horse. However, despite the adversity, she would never allow her passion to be diminished.

A year after the polio, tragedy struck again when her husband of eleven years suffered an unexpected fatal heart attack, leaving her alone to raise three young sons. The years and misfortune gradually sloughed off her easy glamour, giving way to short-cropped, salt-and-pepper gray hair and wasted legs that required the support of a cane or arm-cuff crutches for mobility. Although bereaved and permanently ground bound, she found

Down the Aisle

new strength through her sons and the sanctuary of the sport that she loved.

Even though the boys never shared her equine passion, they moved dutifully from short stirrup ponies to junior show hunters to the hunt field. Flo was an avid motivator whether hobbling along the rail on her cane as a ringside coach or following the hunt field action from the roadways in her burgundy Mercedes as a car hill topper. College provided the boys with a welcome, legitimate excuse to escape from the mandatory equine routine. Much to Flo's disappointment, they never returned to the saddle except for a casual maternal pacification fox hunt on visits home.

Although the boys moved on to non-horse related careers and ponyless families, Flo continued to maintain a personal horse. Her life from childhood had been graced and centered around classic hunters, so she was determined not to let the crippling effects of disease or family disinterest break her tradition. All she required to maintain her status quo was an eager adolescent rider with talent that she could mold to her expectations. With a chosen protégée to pilot her horse in the show ring and hunt field, she could live vicariously through their training and success.

The stable where Flo had boarded her horses throughout the years had originally been built at the turn of the twentieth century as a center for Northshore hunter activities. Flo had maintained a stall on the grounds for two decades before the Captain picked up the lease and opened The Academy. In her day,

Down the Aisle

Flo had experienced the revolving door of management known variously as Royal Elms, Green Tree, Carriage Hill and finally The Academy. Due to the amenities of the facility and the convenience to her home, she had determined to cope with any inconveniences dictated by new management policies. Her well-respected reputation preceded her with each incoming manager who deferred to her expertise and seniority, allowing her to continue her personal training program as long as it did not detract from theirs.

When the Captain took over the facility and implemented his strictly structured European management policies, very few preexisting boarders were tempted to test the rules. Most of the old core opted to move out when the Captain moved in, shipping their horses to barns with more liberal policies.

Flo was one of the few exceptions. She had been ensconced at the end of the second aisle for over 20 years. Her horse and stable routine had been the one dependable constant throughout a turbulent life. In her opinion, the arrival of yet another new barn lessee, albeit a bristly Prussian with a thick accent, was not a serious concern. She had no intention of disrupting her program or interfering with the new management. She just wanted to be left alone to pursue her usual routine.

When I became a student at The Academy stories still abounded in the tack room about the day that the Captain and Mrs. Fromm faced each other from unwavering positions.

Down the Aisle

Although no one had actually overheard the conversation, countless scenarios of the meeting between the two titans had been speculated and blown out of proportion throughout the years. However, several old timers had caught a glimpse of the exchange between his firm brown eyes versus her steely grays that would not, could not, be denied. It was long rumored that the Captain had blinked first because without explanation, Mrs. Fromm was grandfathered in to resume her regular routine without interruption.

From that day forth, Flo's reputation at The Academy was established. While never outwardly unfriendly, she seemed to be surrounded by an invisible, impenetrable fourth wall. When approached, she greeted everyone with the same courteous nod and brief smile then returned to her business, avoiding casual conversation and barn gossip. She was always accompanied by a pair of ancient, grey-muzzled foxhounds who were equally as aloof as their mistress.

I found Flo to be a constant source of interest and admiration. The quality of her horse and the technique of her two-point riding position differed radically from the Captain's deep-seated, three-point military seat. Not only were their training styles different, but there was even a dissimilarity in the appearance of their horses. In contrast to the Captain's sturdy school stock from "out west", Flo's leggy Thoroughbred was the elegant personification of the champion hunters that many of us in the riding school had only seen gracing the pages of magazines like *The Chronicle*.

Ever aware of her environment, Flo grew to admire the proficiency and discipline of the students trained under The Academy system that produced solid, effective riders. As a result, she began to select riders for her horse based upon the Captain's recommendations from his advanced lesson program. It was a tremendous opportunity as the chosen rider was guaranteed all-expense-paid exposure to the "A" circuit show ring as well as the hunt field.

The girl who was lucky enough to be selected to pilot Flo's hunter under her guidance grew immeasurably beyond her old classmates in maturity and elegance. She was given access to the opportunity and horsepower to make an impression in the competitive circles that existed beyond the protected environs of The Academy.

I always savored the opportunity to watch Flo work with her chosen rider. Just like the Captain, she had a no-nonsense training approach that did not encourage two-way communication. In her opinion, her system had been successful for over 40 years, so she saw no reason to open a dialog with a teenager whose primary function was to implement her instructions. But, despite the authoritarian system, the chosen girls always thrived under Flo's tutelage.

Down the Aisle

Students who had achieved advanced jumper class status had to admit feeling a twinge of hope that the next nod to ride Mrs. Fromm's horse would come their way when her current rider graduated out of the junior ranks and headed off to college. However, for me it seemed an unreachable plateau. While Tic-Tac and I had steadily improved and polished our performance, we were both still just graduates from the school string, brimming over with confidence, but lacking finesse and polish in our performance.

However, much to my surprise, my opportunity to reach Academy nirvana came in the spring of my 16th year. Tic-Tac and I had developed and excelled at every challenge presented by the Captain. Although not the flashiest or most athletic pair in the barn, through sheer determination, we had worked our way to the top of every exercise, no matter how demanding.

Tic-Tac gave me the confidence to soar!

Down the Aisle

While we had become dependable technicians of the stadium course, we thrived on the long galloping lines that carried us gleefully around the solid coops, logs and banks of the back field cross-country course. My prowess and timing had recently earned me the opportunity to be chosen to test drive some of the newly arrived "out west" horses. The Captain had even hinted at the prospect of my becoming a Summer Camp low level instructor in the upcoming season.

I thought my junior riding career was as good as it could get until I noticed that Mrs. Fromm had begun to take an interest in me. During several lessons, I had noticed her leaning on the fence, intently watching my progress while talking quietly to the Captain who would occasionally nod in my direction.

A few weeks later the Captain stopped outside my stall while I was grooming Tic-Tac. "Birdie, an opportunity may be available for you to ride for Mrs. Fromm. You have done a very good job with your training and have earned this reward. It may open future doors for you in the sport. I think it is something to seriously consider."

Three days later I found myself leading Mrs. Fromm's elegant mahogany bay gelding, Cleanex, up to the mounting block for a test ride. I slipped my foot nervously into the stirrup, savoring the soft touch of the pliable leather of the Stubben saddle that had graced the backs of her horses long before I was born. She watched

Down the Aisle

quietly while I adjusted the leathers, and then nodded for me to follow her to the outdoor arena.

Whatever nerves had iced my hands and dried out my mouth were dispelled as soon as I legged the bold gelding into a forward canter around the track. Those long, easy strides opened up an extraordinary new world of feel within my hands and legs. He was smooth as silk and totally responsive to my slightest aids. Until that moment, I don't think I ever truly understood what Dad meant when he had quipped that there was no comparison between his practical blue Ford Galaxy versus the red Corvette Stingray of his dreams.

I studiously concentrated on Flo's instructions that directed me through basic flatwork on to single cross rails, building to a serious four-foot combination. With each new challenge, I silently thanked the Captain for the opportunity he had given me to catch-ride so many unfamiliar horses, each requiring me to quickly assess and adjust to their needs without hesitation.

The audition ride clicked as though we had been a seasoned pair for months. "Well done," Mrs. Fromm finally approved, smiling for the first time. "He's a grand fellow, my Cleanex. Seemed to get on with you alright. With some work and polish I think you might work for me. Time will tell. I'm willing to give it a go if you're willing to dedicate yourself to make the necessary effort, Leslie."

Down the Aisle

It was the first time that anyone at the stable had addressed me by my proper name since the Captain had coined the nickname "Birdie". It seemed to signify a new beginning for me as Flo tentatively invited me into her private, guarded world.

Due to her generosity and connections, I found myself thrust into the privileged world of "A" circuit hunters and the timeworn traditions of hunt field stirrup cups that had previously existed beyond my dreams and my parents' means. Depending upon the season, I would find myself sharply turned out in full hunt appointments supplied by Mrs. Fromm to tackle the challenge of the Corinthian hunter course at the Lake Forest Horse Show; or, at the end of a busy show season, galloping pell-mell aboard Cleanex in the first flight of the Mill Creek Hunt field. We would charge breathlessly over frozen turf, cheeks flushed pink from the chill and snow flakes across my skin while Flo tried to keep the field in sight from behind the wheel of her burgundy Mercedes, leading the car hill toppers across the country roads.

Despite her demanding schedule for Cleanex, she always made sure I had time to pursue my personal training of Tic-Tac. Although my sturdy little horse lacked the physical scope and style to compete at Cleanex's level, he and I benefited greatly from exposure to Flo's techniques.

In the beginning, it was only my place to listen and try to implement her detailed instructions. However, as time progressed, our relationship slowly matured to a level beyond pupil and mentor

Down the Aisle

as my tenacity to excel earned first her respect and then her friendship. As the days and months passed, we began to generate our own personal history founded on a true horse lover's rapport that recognized no age barriers.

***Cleanex and I share show course highlights
with Flo and my mother.***

Whatever the season, on Mondays when the stable was closed, we would reconvene to the cozy, wood-paneled library of her home to review the previous week's work and set new goals for the next. Flo would sip Makers Mark on the rocks while I drank Coke from fox head etched glasses. We would sit in the

Down the Aisle

deep, red leather arm chairs sharing endless hours of serious horse talk while her foxhounds curled up to snore at our feet. Her world became my special sanctuary where day-to-day adolescent uncertainties would rock away in the cradle of our equine dialog.

All too soon I outgrew the junior ranks and my ride on Cleanex. However, even when I headed off for college and beyond, I never left Flo far behind. Whenever I returned home to visit, my first stop was always Flo's library where I sought to rediscover the sanctuary of her companionship that existed in the warm bonds of horse talk and the smell of leather and old foxhounds.

Throughout the years of our relationship, Flo dressed me in her experiences in addition to her well-worn, beloved hunt appointments. Her bone-handled whip with the leather lash and blue popper still hangs in my mud room long after its last crack to bring an errant foxhound in check. Next to it is a black-and-white picture of Cleanex and me easily airing a huge log pile in the Working Hunter Stakes at the Dunham Woods horse show. In the photo, I'm wearing Flo's black velvet hunt cap and a mile wide grin that I know she was sharing from her usual vantage point.

Down the Aisle

Cleanex and I airing the stacked logs at Dunham Woods.

Down the Aisle

Chapter Five
Spellbinder

For me, no season can compare with the crisp bite of fall. As a child somersaulting into musty, raked leaf piles with my cocker, Taffy, or collecting monarchs from the neighbor's butterfly bush were memorable diversions. High on my list of favorites were carving jack-o-lanterns with Dad or trick-or-treating in a fantasy "wanna be" costume.

My preferred costumes all revolved around horses. Over the years, I paraded as everything equine-related from a tiny, pink-winged princess hugging my best plush bedtime charger to an Indian with a three-foot tall cardboard cut-out Pinto that Dad would lug along as he chaperoned me from door-to-door treat stops. When I was enrolled at The Academy, I would proudly masquerade on Beggar's Night in my horse show finery. My disguise was that of an Olympian with a picture of my current favorite team horse pasted onto my goodie bag. If questioned by a curious treat giver, I could rapid fire recite my dream horse's competition stats without hesitation.

Down the Aisle

As my years lengthened, the fall season gained new focus. I eagerly anticipated the fresh chill of a frosty morning against my cheek as the air settled over the damp earth whose fields had recently given up their rich harvest of corn and soybeans. The full autumn pallet of red, burgundy and gold added seasoning to the tree lined horizons that bordered the fields I roamed. In harmony with the changing season, I loved to listen to the hollow music of migrating geese that glided through the mist rising off a secluded meadow pond. To experience all this from the back of a trusted horse was total sensory heaven.

Add to the mix the bay of a pack of working foxhounds in full cry, hot on the line of a crafty fox. In close pursuit rumbled the charge of the hunt field, scrambling down banks, splashing through icy creeks and soaring over paneled coops focused on staying close to the action. Their breathtaking dash only pauses momentarily when the keen noses of the hounds need to be recast for a misplaced scent of their elusive quarry. Steam rises from the damp hair on the backs of the horses which mingles with the melton wool coats of their riders. Nostrils flare and snort while hooves shuffle and strike out with impatience at what seems an interminable length to the check.

"B-r-r-r, B-r-r-r," the senior bitch in the pack sounds a high pitched cry of discovery from the far end of the covert.

Down the Aisle

"T-r-r, T-r-r," answers the huntsman's horn, cheering on his most reliable girl, urging the rest of the pack to jump on her line as they tear out of the covert as one.

In a moment, the entire field is off again in hot pursuit of the line they will joyously chase until the horses or the day run out. Then it's back to the stable, hacking down dirt roads with good friends on favored companions whose tired ears still prick if an errant hound gives a final bit of tongue. The camaraderie builds new memories of fresh exploits to be rehashed and embellished over hot buttered rum and marshmallow laced cups of cocoa shared round a roaring fire in the clubhouse after the horses are cooled out and put up for the day.

I was totally immersed in this paradise my final year of high school. No matter the weather, I hunted every Wednesday and Saturday through mid-December or until the Lake Michigan snows came too early or deep for the hounds to go out. I had even arranged my school schedule to permit me to partake in the early morning weekday hunts as long as I was back in class by 10 a.m.

The black shuttered, white clapboard hunt club stable became my second home during the season. Built in the shape of a horse shoe with a gated entrance at the top, each of the 26 stalls had dutch doors that opened onto a spacious courtyard where the horses and hounds gathered on hunting mornings. In the back center of the courtyard stood a white frame single story house,

Down the Aisle

divided between members' club and the huntsman's personal home.

On days that the hounds did not go out, after school I would make the thirty minute drive up to the hunt club to hack out cross country on Cleanex. I relished the free access to miles of open fields and woodlands that could easily be gained via the coops that paneled the hunt country. It was a delicious sense of absolute freedom to be able to take off in any direction at any speed without any itinerary. In hindsight, it probably was not the safest or most sensible agenda as no one knew where I had disappeared into the thousands of potential acres. However, I always managed to work my way back to the stable by dark in an age of youth where the mantel of invincibility often replaced common sense.

Thanks to Flo and the opportunities she had afforded me, my life had developed a singular equine rhythm from which I never hoped to fall out of sync. The only low point had come the previous June when my dear Tic-Tac had sustained an injury to his right stifle joint while playing during turn-out. Despite prompt veterinary attention, it had resulted in a slight, permanent lameness. While the condition would not prevent him from continuing to enjoy light work and trail riding, it was obvious that my jumping aspirations for him would have to be curtailed.

For the first time in my short life, my shield of indomitability gained a little tarnish as I was confronted by the hard lesson of facing unexpected, uncontrollable limitations. My mentors had made me a student of the positive thinking school whose mantra was if one worked hard enough, any hurdle no matter how daunting could eventually be surmounted. However, despite my protestations and administrations, the veterinarians assured my parents in no uncertain terms that Tic-Tac's performance career was over.

Leave it to Flo to take charge and keep everyone moving forward on the track that she deemed in her infinite wisdom to be appropriate. Before I could saturate too many boxes of tissue, she had found Tic-Tac the ideal retirement home with an old friend in Barrington Hills who had been searching for a dependable companion horse for light trail riding. The woman owned a five-acre farm with a cute 2-stall barn that opened onto a big grassy pasture. Her husband rode a chunky, grey Quarter Horse who would be Tic-Tac's pasture mate. It was the perfect fit for everyone with the best part being that I could visit whenever I wanted.

My parents were delighted with the plan. With college looming in the near future, it seemed the perfect solution. They felt relieved of the dilemma of having to separate me from my beloved Tic-Tac when the time came to leave for school and finally put the responsibilities of higher education and a future career ahead of my childhood passion for horses.

In their eyes, the uncertain road ahead had been eased with Flo's sensible solution. My future path was now set to move

Down the Aisle

smoothly on to the next natural level. That was until Spellbinder arrived at the hunt club stable and cast her magic over all of us.

Ben Norman, the club's resident professional Irish huntsman, liked to speculate on the occasional off-the-track sales horse. Over the years he had cultivated a dependable trackside agent to sniff out interesting prospects that could be picked up at a discount then retrained for a comfortable profit to bolster his salary from the club. Rather than risk his middle-aged neck on the rank youngsters, he would oversee his teenage daughter legging them up to take off the rough edges. While Casey Norman was not a stylish rider, she could master any whirlwind with a balance and resolve that imparted confidence in the new prospects. Once basic manners and the first glimmer of potential were evident, Ben would then propose them to appropriate club members as future show or hunt prospects.

Spellbinder arrived at the hunt club direct from Arlington Park where she had just completed her second season of racing. The big, bay mare was bred to the hilt, but judging from her record, she had inherited more conformation than speed from her ancestors' gene pool. Two seconds, four thirds and nothing to show in the win column over two seasons of trying meant it was time to head for an alternative performance career or the breeding shed.

She was a handsome, big boned mare without a white hair on her solid bay, 16.3 hand frame. The full eyes that looked

Down the Aisle

out from her elegant head were veiled as only a mare's can be. Her early days at the club were spent gazing out over the stall dutch door into the stable yard, so detached that it was difficult to read her emotions.

From the moment of her arrival, I was fascinated by this striking mare who was stabled two stalls down from Cleanex. Her mystery and aloofness were an irresistible draw. I was even more challenged to make a connection when she resisted acknowledging the carrot and sugar enticements that I offered.

The slightest human overtures into her space evoked an immediate "Back off, lady" response. Her message was clearly expressed through pinned ears, a sharp click of snapping teeth, and an emphatic kick of the stall wall. But, rather than feeling rebuffed, I was even more motivated to drive a friendly wedge into her formidable demeanor.

Although her inhospitable stall manners put off prospective clients, if they had only waited to see her move, they would have realized that she came alive under saddle. While in her stall she gave off negative vibes to anyone who made eye contact, in movement she was sheer joy with ears pricked sharply forward seeking the next horizon. Spellbinder's pure, expressive movement powered by long, flowing strides was guaranteed to take the breath away from any horse lover.

Ben Norman's daughter was a tough, athletic rider, but even Casey had her hands and concentration full in the early days

Down the Aisle

aboard the mare. It required all her skills to sit tight against the leaping, plunging bay whirlwind whose singular focus was to get out of the stall and gallop.

Flo agreed with my enthusiastic appraisal as we watched Casey breeze the mare around the perimeter of the jump field one bright October afternoon. "You're absolutely right, Leslie. She's an outstanding young prospect. It'll take a little extra skill to get the job done, but it's very possible with the right rider. Whoever succeeds in getting through that wall of resistance will find herself with a real prize."

Buoyed by Flo's encouragement, I fixated on winning that prize for myself. The first stage of my plan was to earn the mare's confidence. Gradually, ever so gradually, I noticed a flicker of recognition when I approached her stall, carrot bribe in hand and an inviting coo in my voice. With time and patience, the recognition slowly grew to acknowledgement that finally rewarded me with an ever so soft nicker.

It didn't take long for Ben Norman's horse dealer sixth sense to zero in on my chemistry with Spellbinder. "That mare likes you, she does," he declared one afternoon when he caught me slipping carrot chunks into her muzzle that lingered a little longer than necessary in my palm. "I haven't seen her take to anyone quite like that not even Casey. Maybe it's time you get to know her a little better from on top."

Down the Aisle

I caught my breath at the offer that I'd been waiting to hear.

"Casey's down with a bit of a cold," he continued. "But, I hate to let the mare stand a day. She needs regular work to keep the edge off. You're certainly up to the job, so how about it? I think you'll find she's got something special."

That was all the invitation I needed. The teaser at the end wasn't necessary to encourage me. I already knew she was something special. Before he could reconsider, I was off to the tack room, setting a new land speed record to gather brushes, pad, boots and tack.

When she was groomed and tacked, Ben gave me a light leg up onto the saddle. Immediately upon feeling my weight, Spellbinder began to paw and impatiently flip her head. Ben kept hold of the reins, walking us in a big circle to try to relax her while he imparted final instructions.

"She's a bit headstrong, this lass," he cautioned, stroking the mare to calm her. "Likes to take a hold. Be sure you keep a deep seat and don't let her pull you out of the bridle. Stay at the trot until you get a feel for her."

"I've got a good idea what she needs from watching Casey's sessions," I assured him. "But I promise to take it slow until we get to know each other."

Ben patted my thigh. For a moment, I remembered Dad's confidence building touch as we circled the Richardson's pony

Down the Aisle

ring so many years earlier, but the memory was fleeting as Spellbinder impatiently tried to snatch the reins out of Ben's firm grip.

"She's track fit and may be a lot more horse than you expect," the huntsman advised. "Take it slow and easy. Let me know what you think when you get back."

My pent up eagerness to experience the mare's talents carried me jigging and skittering out of the courtyard toward the back hunt field without a second thought. It didn't take long to realize that Ben was right. I had definitely never experienced from the irons so much raw power that was offered by this horse fresh off the track. Regrettably, I also quickly realized that her very green status did not include an operator's manual.

In contrast to the light, responsive mouths of the hunters I had previously ridden, this track horse had been trained to bear down and lean against the bit when running. Unlike those dependable hunters who had patiently served as my classroom, this raw mare definitely lacked power steering as well as brakes – an important combination that required an immediate adjustment to assure self-preservation.

Spellbinder was not in the least bit concerned about my personal space or comfort. When I asked her to step up into a trot, she impatiently grabbed the bit and took off in a gallop. All she wanted to do was run for the sheer joy of the freedom of

Down the Aisle

movement. I sensed she didn't care whether or not I went just as long as I stayed balanced in the saddle and out of her way.

Her strides opened up so quickly that the rush of wind across my cheeks brought tears to my eyes. As we flew across the field in a breakneck gallop, it only took a moment to realize that she was totally unresponsive to any of my insistent turning and stopping aids. It was small comfort to sense that we were traveling far too fast for her to throw in a buck. Aside from bailing out which was not an attractive option at high speed, I had no recourse but to drop my heels and close my hip angle, deepening my seat in the saddle as I struggled for security. As an added precaution, I grabbed a handful of her thick black mane to further stabilize my balance.

When I finally stopped fighting the bit, I realized that she was actually settling into a rhythm. While not any slower, at least it hinted at a regularity that I could follow through my arms and back. Gradually, I gained a glimmer of confidence, feeling myself being drawn in by the mare's contagious enthusiasm for speed.

It was exhilarating. As my fear abated, I started laughing unable to stop for the pure thrill. At the sound of my voice, for a brief moment Spellbinder's strides hesitated, her ears flipping back toward me as though surprised. Then, just as quickly, she lurched even more forward in a bold surge. But by this time, I was a willing partner, urging her on with every fiber of my body that moments earlier I had sought to restrict. Faster, now even faster over the

Down the Aisle

undulating ground that carried us farther and farther away from the hunt club.

We were both blowing and sweating profusely when she finally dropped down into a trot then into a walk of her own accord. Gone was the jig of nervous anticipation. Her strides fell into a long, sweeping motion that glided easily over the ground. The reins that had earlier been taut with tension slipped casually through my fingers to the buckle as I easily turned her for the long ride back to the stable.

I stroked the sweat-lathered brown neck, sensing that my joy was equally shared. With a snort at my touch, she lowered her neck, head bobbing in rhythm as she took deep, full breaths to regain her wind.

Now, in relaxation, I could asses her many qualities that went far beyond a talent for speed and power. She was a perfect fit for me, filling up my leg as well as my heart. I realized her temperament that had put off so many was only a protective shell hiding a remarkable heart and soul. I knew that with time I could capture her spirit. The prospect of custom molding such a talent from scratch was a thrilling challenge.

However, I knew it would not take much longer for Casey's training program to improve the mare's rideability. Then, I realized it would only be a matter of time until Spellbinder's market value increased proportionately, pricing her beyond my reach. If I was to possess my dream horse it would have to happen very soon

Down the Aisle

while potential buyers still eyed her with skeptical raised eyebrows.

The biggest hurdle would be overcoming the parental obstacle. To this point in my short equine career, their support could not be faulted. My parents had made my equine obsession a family project, rarely missing a show or weekend hunt meet. They had even made a serious effort to stay current on my lessons and the terminology in an attempt to offer feedback. Countless summer family weekends had been sacrificed to the heat, bugs and dust that came with showing, standing shoulder-to-shoulder with Flo to cheer me over another post-and-rail course.

However, as they never failed to remind me, college was just around the corner and deferment to pursue a riding career was not a negotiable option. In their minds, the sale of Tic-Tac represented the end of our family's horse ownership era with college the new priority. Unfortunately, this was the one time that I could not depend upon Flo as an ally as she was equally adamant about the necessity of securing a college degree no matter the direction of my future work path. My only hope to move my plan for Spellbinder forward was to create some wiggle room with my parents on the horse ownership side of the equation.

My fingers stroked the neck muscling that arched over the mare's beautiful topline. "There has to be a way," I vowed with the determination of my favorite movie heroine, Scarlet O'Hara.

Down the Aisle

I took a handful of her thick mane with the same resolve that Scarlet had when she clutched that handful of dirt from the fields of her beloved Tara, the O'Hara family plantation in the movie classic *Gone with the Wind*. I envisioned Scarlet defiantly shaking her fist at the sky and uttering her famous declaration, "As God is my witness, I will never go hungry again!"

While my cause was not quite as desperate, I was determined to overcome this current obstacle that blocked the path I envisioned down my aisle. My emotions were equally as resolute as Scarlett's as my fingers closed tightly around the mare's coarse hair. "As God is my witness, there will be a way!"

Chapter Six
Beneath the Ivy

In the fall of 1968, Spellbinder and I were officially enrolled as freshmen beneath the ivy covered walls of Stephens College in Columbia, Missouri. Flo had introduced me to the female liberal arts college complete with 50 stall stable and an equine studies department. It was the perfect fit for a horse-crazy adolescent who would much prefer a career riding horses than climb the hallowed rungs of higher education.

However, the one aspect of academia that had always appealed to me was the creative arts. Stephens College offered strong departments in that area with excellent field experienced professors, so it seemed the perfect fit. In addition to four years of active involvement in my high school's theater department, I had also excelled in creative writing. The ability to combine these interests without abandoning my equine passion made Stephens an attractive choice.

I never for a moment lost track of how miraculously lucky I was to own Spellbinder let alone take her with me to college. To this day, I don't think my parents realized what hit them when they came under Flo's and my one-two hard sell punch to seal the deal on the purchase of Spellbinder. Totally captivated by the big mare's potential, we were not to be denied by letting her slip into someone else's hands as her talents blossomed. Using our own brand of logic and financial incentive, we worked together on a convincing argument to sway my parents.

Flo proved to be the consummate equine saleswoman. Commercializing on my parent's respect for her years of experience, she positioned her argument to represent the mare as the ideal opportunity for me to progress to the next level. According to Flo's reasoning, Spellbinder would provide me with the chance to develop a quality young prospect from scratch, thus allowing me to make my first training mark in the sport.

When my parents raised dubious eyebrows over the limited extent of my experience, Flo was quick to reassure them that it would be her pleasure to oversee the entire training process. She would make it her priority to protect my wellbeing as well as their financial investment. The lucrative angle of her sales pitch to my parents was the promise of financial return. They listened carefully as Flo explained that once Spellbinder was satisfactorily trained to competition level, the mare would represent an excellent return on their initial investment. Barring unforeseen circumstances, the future value of the mare should offset some of my looming college expenses.

Down the Aisle

My part was to assume the role of adoring daughter upon whom Dad had always found it extremely difficult to deny. A bit manipulative Flo and I agreed, but fair game considering the prize that was at stake. My mother, on the other hand, was not as soft a touch to her daughter's charms. She had always been the cautious parent, seeking to keep the family anchored in a safe harbor whereas if Dad had his druthers, he would have sailed out in a leaky craft just to taste the salt air upon his lips.

However, once Dad was on board with our grand plan, it was only a matter of time until my mother reluctantly acquiesced, finally hooked by the tempting bait of the investment prospects. But even in acceptance, she issued a mandatory ultimatum to which we all had to agree before the plan could move forward. Her terms dictated that the proposed equine investment must be cashed in prior to my college start date or there would be no deal. "Understood?!?"

Guided by Flo's expertise and my dedication, Spellbinder blossomed into more than any of us could have hoped as she progressed from raw, headstrong training prospect into dependable show ring champion in the esteemed conformation hunter division. While her value swelled with each winning ride, so did my attachment and determination to perpetuate our relationship.

Down the Aisle

My proud Dad the day he purchased Spellbinder for me.

But as the saying goes, even the best laid plans are meant to change. And fortunately, so did my mother's once unwavering position that the mare must be sold before the start of college. I was never quite certain of the true rationale for her 180-degree reversal, but I gladly accepted the revised ground rules that found Spellbinder heading south to Stephens College with me in September, 1968.

However, in order to preserve my equine status quo, my mother's new ultimatum dictated that I maintain a minimum 3-point grade average in a curriculum that extended beyond stable management courses to core subjects. My parents would

Down the Aisle

reevaluate my educational productivity at the end of each semester. Never had I had so much motivation to hit the books.

Stephens College was a nine hour drive from my home in Deerfield, Illinois. Freshman year represented my first long solo foray. With no direct flights from campus and a three hour Trailways bus ride to the nearest major commercial airport in St. Louis, a visit home to ease the loneliness required a concerted coordination of time and travel modes.

During my first semester, Spellbinder's inherent value increased more as a companion to cheer me and chase away the blues than an elite training partner. Her welcoming nicker helped to soften the separation anxiety that I initially experienced away from family, friends and my hometown honey. My mare was usually successful in eradicating my homesickness on all counts except the hometown honey.

Jeff and I started dating in 1967 in the fall of our senior year at Deerfield High School during the production of Student Stunts. The annual variety show featured music, dance and comedy skits developed by the senior class. Loving all things theatrical, I had auditioned as a dancer while Jeff had landed a solo singing act, playing his guitar to the poignant Glen Yarborough love song "Until It's Time for You to Go."

Irene Kominski, English teacher turned musical revue director for Stunts, was a true romantic. She had a natural show business knack for knowing what made the best theater. With

Down the Aisle

Jeff's hip propped casually against an old wooden stool stage left, he and his 12-string guitar filled the theater with the promise of love lost. Silhouetted on stage behind a filmy scrim, I danced an ethereal solo to his strum that touched adolescent hearts all the way to the back row of the auditorium. There was no doubt that our act worked its magic not only on the audience, but on us as well.

No teenage girl's journey down the barn aisle would be complete without the specter of first love which often results in an unavoidable romantic detour from the stable. Fueled by the initial hormonal stirrings that tend to turn an adolescent's normal world upside down, this is often the first real test of a horse lover's dedication. Romantic deviations can take the inconvenient form of a mere speed bump or the total disappearance into a relationship labyrinth in which the four-legged passion is forever transferred to a two-legged preference.

Despite total immersion in a demanding equine training schedule, my hormones were not immune to adolescent urges. Jeff and I were quickly swallowed up by a mad, crazy passion made even stronger since it was first love for both of us. It was obvious to all our friends and family that we had something more serious than the usual high school crush. At the end of our senior year, our classmates even voted us "Couple Most Likely to Stay Together."

Down the Aisle

Jeff was over the top in love with me. He didn't care where we spent our time as long as it was together. My heart, on the other hand, was torn between the raging hormones ignited by his touch and the adrenalin rush of my training time aboard Spellbinder. Jeff's devotion must have been a little stronger than mine. Although he loved the golf course and his guitar, our path more often led to the barn or a horse show.

While the incentive of taking my mare to college influenced my decision to select Stephens College, Jeff's more serious academic goals guided him to DePauw University in Greencastle, Indiana. Two states and six hours of separation were almost too much to bear. At Jeff's urging, I had briefly considered DePauw, but the bottom line was it lacked a stable and a way to stay connected to my mare. To remain within Jeff's world, I would have had to sell Spellbinder. While I teetered on the brink of that decision, I just wasn't ready to make the ultimate sacrifice.

In hindsight, separate college choices may have actually been the deciding factor in my parents relenting to allow me to keep my mare. I think that they felt Jeff and I had gotten too serious too fast. A wedge of distance and time seemed the ideal solution to both sets of parents who hoped the relationship would cool down.

However, there is much truth to the old saying that absence makes the heart grow fonder. As the days and weeks between us lengthened, I found that rather then diminishing, my feelings for

Down the Aisle

Jeff deepened. For the first time in my life, the longings of my romantic heart won out over the devotion of my equine heart.

After two years of college campus separation, I sensed that Jeff was drawing away from me into the new life he was carving for himself at DePauw. When the hint of "another woman friend" began to raise its threatening head in our phone conversations, I realized that he needed more than I could offer from the distance that separated us. It was time to seriously consider transferring if our relationship had any hope of survival.

I sensed that my adult future lay with this man who encompassed my heart and mind every day of our separation. Despite every conceivable creative scenario, I could see no way to bridge the distance between us and, at the same time, keep Spellbinder. While I knew I could always find a way to have horses in my life, I realized that I needed to temporarily consider a more traditional non-equine aisle if I were to salvage my relationship with Jeff.

Sadly, I accepted the reality that it was time to move my life forward toward beckoning adulthood. It was time to cash in on the investment that my parents had made in Spellbinder. With great reluctance, I placed the inevitable "For Sale" ad in *The Chronicle of the Horse*.

As soon as the ad hit displaying Spellbinder's picture and resume, it generated responses from across the country. I dreaded the approaching day that I would have to show my mare to

Down the Aisle

prospective buyers. However, there was one respondent who offered a glimmer of hope to my dilemma. Dick Carter was an architect who owned a small farm in Carmel, Indiana, where he kept ponies for his three children as well as hunt horses for himself and his wife. While fox hunting was his passion, he was looking to upgrade to a made "A" circuit hunter to compete during the off-season. When I checked Carmel's location on a map, I found to my delight that it was only 1 ½ hours from Greencastle where I would be transferring to DePauw in September to begin my junior year.

From childhood, at times of decision or crisis, I had often sensed a strong surrounding presence that seemed to guide my journey down the many aisles I traversed. While some people pass this feeling off as instinct or intuition, many of my wondrous experiences as well as last minute avoidance of pitfalls seemed to spring from a much stronger source. I believed I had the free will to fly, but I sensed that if I soared too high or faltered upon looking down, there was the guiding energy of a Guardian Spirit ready to right my course if I would just pause to listen.

I was keenly aware of this guidance when I scheduled Dick Carter's try-out ride on my mare. He was a tall, angular man with a red head's pasty complexion beneath buzz cut hair. Spellbinder's conformation and athleticism immediately hooked him as I jumped her around a course for his scrutiny. Even though

Down the Aisle

he tried to present a serious, all business façade, I could tell he was salivating for a test drive.

Although he rode with the manufactured precision of one who has come to the saddle in their middle years rather than with the easy flow of a childhood spent in the irons, Spellbinder did nothing to diminish his anticipation. She accommodated his stiffness with calm and grace, packing him safely over any fence he steered her toward.

All too soon it was a done deal with only the prepurchase exam standing between me and separation from my beloved mare. However, my Guardian Spirit once again stepped to the forefront with an unexpected offer from the prospective buyer. When Dick Carter learned I would be heading off to DePauw, he suggested I consider commuting to his farm several days a week to help him and Spellbinder make the transition to their new partnership. There would also be the opportunity to instruct his wife and children. Although his offer didn't lessen the impact of Spellbinder's sale, it afforded me the chance to stay connected with my mare.

The handover date was set for mid-August at the Barrington Horse Show. Dick and Lynn Carter as well as the three little Carters wanted to witness their new purchase in action. Spellbinder didn't disappoint, earning a stall front covered in blue ribbons, culminating in our final tri-color championship in the Regular Working Hunter division.

Down the Aisle

The final jump of my final show with Spellbinder

There was much celebrating by the Carter clan as they dressed my mare in a new double-stitched halter with a shiny brass nameplate bearing Dick Carter's name beneath Spellbinder's. Legs carefully wrapped in the navy bandages of the Carter farm colors, my mare obediently loaded into her new trailer without hesitation. I felt like I was watching the departure of the bridge that had carried me over the turbulence of adolescence without feeling certain that I had yet reached the security of the other side. Even though I knew I would be fortunate to see and work with her again in a few brief weeks, sadly, it would be under someone else's name and control.

As the trailer pulled out of the show grounds with the Carters all gaily waving from the windows, Jeff wrapped his arm

Down the Aisle

comfortingly around my shoulders. I was grateful for the support he had offered throughout the show to help ease my sadness at Spellbinder's departure. However, as I felt his hug tighten, I momentarily wondered if it would be enough to replace the void I was feeling.

While Jeff ignited my passion of the heart, when I began classes at DePauw, Professor Christman ignited my passion for the pen. Elizabeth Christman had spent the majority of her career as a top literary agent. Based in New York City, she had years of experience connecting promising writers with major publishing houses. Burned out in her early fifties by the pressures of the publishing business, she signed on as an associate English professor at DePauw, fulfilling her longtime dream of working with aspiring university composition students.

An unassuming, single woman who seemed content to push back as far as possible from the hectic New York lifestyle, she had rented a second floor apartment in a 1940's stucco bungalow within walking distance of campus. The walls of her study where she counseled writing students were covered with framed covers of books whose contracts she had negotiated. The impressive literary display was not lost on my aspirations as I started an independent creative writing study project.

The composition assignment focused on the development of an original story line into a novel format. Throughout the course, we met every Tuesday and Friday from 2 – 4 p.m. in her cozy

Down the Aisle

apartment that she felt was more conducive to stimulating creativity in aspiring writers than the file cabinet-sized office assigned to her in Asbury Hall. In those productive sessions, I learned the ground rules of professional writing, elevating my skills from the proverbial romantic candle-in-the-attic style to a clear, precise commercial technique.

"Write what you know. Know what you write." had been drilled into me from my earliest composition classes. Taking that advice to heart, it was an obvious choice that my project for Professor Christman chronicled the early exploits of a young adolescent living out the dream of her burgeoning equine passion. Aptly titled **Tic-Tac**, the finished manuscript won the respect of my professor. So much so that she generously used her connections to help me gain a contract with Dodd, Mead and Company's juvenile book division with publication scheduled for September following my graduation from DePauw.

The day Professor Christman proudly presented me with the signed publisher's contract was unforgettable. After a childhood spent reading every imaginable book written about horses, it was humbling to realize that my personally penned story would join the bookshelves of a whole new generation of horse lovers. Readers for years to come would cherish and remember the story of my Tic-Tac and the magical world of The Academy in the same way I treasured **The Horsemasters**, **A Horse of Her Own**, and **Casey Jones Rides Vanity**.

Down the Aisle

The aisle I traveled down during my college years often diverged into uncharted territory. As graduation loomed, between the book deal, my ability to maintain a connection for two extra years with my beloved Spellbinder, topped off by a looming October wedding date with my now fiancé Jeff, life seemed to have made a satisfactory course correction.

Dad beamed with pride on graduation day as he gave me a big hug. "Gosh, I envy you for all that's ahead, Les. You must be happy as a clam at high tide."

Logically, I knew I should share his exuberance. In Dad's eyes, I was graduating not just from college, but graduating into the next stage of my adult life. Moving out into the opportunities of the real world with sheepskin in hand and a committed relationship with Jeff soon to be consecrated should have filled me with satisfaction. But, that big step forward also meant leaving behind the remnants of my relationship with Spellbinder without the prospect of another special mount to take her place. So, although my hands were full of the promise of all that lay ahead, I couldn't help but feel a great void where my fingers no longer closed around my own set of reins.

Down the Aisle

Chapter Seven
Crimson Rust

Crimson Rust was the essence of classic Thoroughbred conformation and bloodlines. Aptly named for the radiance of a deep chestnut coat, his striking presence was accentuated by four short white socks and the distinctive facial markings of a perfect star and snip that set off his chiseled head. Although measuring on the low side of average at 16.0 hands, his slender legs and arched neck created a distinctive elegance that seemed to stand him above taller horses.

Descended from the hallowed racing genes of the illustrious War Admiral and Man O' War, he moved in a restless state of energy that optimistic observers attributed to a core of speed inherited from his notable bloodlines. It was easy to see why hopeful idealists believed he was blessed with the ability to lap the field or jump the moon.

Crimson Rust's early career was forged upon the track aspirations of a dream chaser newly infected with the thrill of racing. Initially hooked by the gelding's flashy pedigree and the untested bravado of a fledgling trainer eager to build a client base,

Down the Aisle

it only took an expensive season of poor results to sour the owner's enthusiasm. Within a year of the initial investment, his budget plus slush fund had been depleted with nothing to prop up the dream except two third place finishes and a growing pile of debt. By the end of the season, his shiny crimson prospect had dwindled from the highest of expectations to a fire sale property on the block to the top bidder.

While Crimson Rust's track future was greatly diminished, four clean legs and a deeply discounted price made him an irresistible temptation for a young bride with a minimal budget that overflowed with dreams of a new equine partner.

I was testament to the fact that even a marriage of passion and the soul is not a cure for a full blown case of horse fever. The connection between ardent horse lover and the heart of a horse is too strong a bond for mere mortal love to break.

Even back in my college days as I was placing ads to sell my beloved Spellbinder, I had never made a secret to family or fiancé of my intent to purchase another horse as soon as circumstances warranted. My mother had been certain that a good marriage would awaken "adult" sensibilities to reprioritize my life into what she considered a more normal mode. In her mind, while equine pursuits had represented an acceptable outlet that fostered responsibility in my youth, with maturity and college graduation should come commitment to what she considered a "real world" career and family building. Dad, on the other hand,

Down the Aisle

while not willing to openly contradict my mother, had always recognized the lifelong magnitude of my affliction which had originated in our shared afternoon pony ride escapes with Jambalaya.

I had assumed that upon graduation our individual careers would develop in our home base of Chicago. Surrounded by family and friends, it promised to be a mutually nurturing environment for our blossoming relationship. Although my heart was still in the stable, I felt I owed it to my parents to attempt a traditional career path in appreciation of their four year college investment in my future.

Soon after graduation, my career expectations were jolted by a real world reality check. Assuming that my recently inked book contract with Dodd, Mead & Company would give me a leg up on the competition, I had planned to use my communications degree to pursue a career in Chicago's education-based publishing market. However, it quickly became clear as I made the interview rounds that in order to be considered for hire even as an editorial assistant, a degree in education or previous publishing experience from the editorial side of the desk was a prerequisite.

Jeff had planned on pursuing an on-air radio career. The final two years in college he had anchored "McDonald in the Morning" weekdays on WGRE, the campus radio station. Unfortunately, it didn't take him long to realize that there were very limited on-air opportunities for recent college grads that paid

Down the Aisle

a living wage. The only viable option was to explore outside his desired field for a career that promised growth and challenge. A multitude of interviews resulted in the management training program at Sears as his top choice.

Jeff and I wrestled long hours contemplating the life-altering prospects of a career with Sears. The one certainty of an employee's corporate success with the company was the guarantee of regular relocation transfers. The average stay per assignment was three – five years, even shorter for a manager on a fast promotional track.

All that was well and good for Jeff whose efforts would be rewarded with personal growth from a burgeoning career. However, from my side of the equation, it boded non-existent job security with scant opportunity to build my own career due to the uprooting frequency of Jeff's mandatory moves. If I agreed to his career choice, I would also be obliged to move far from the embrace of family and friends. While I didn't want to squelch his ambitions, I was having difficulty finding a self-fulfilling light at the end of the aisle in which I now found myself.

We finally reached an agreement when Jeff promised that if I was willing to be flexible to his frequent job transfers that really translated to mean being career transient for the next several decades, he would find a way to help me stay in the saddle on my own horse. And, with that unexpected vow, the door was flung wide open for my much desired horse purchase.

Down the Aisle

I sensed a nudge from my Guardian Spirit at the peak of this personal turmoil when the first hint of Crimson Rust appeared. It was only a small classified ad in the Sunday Chicago Tribune, but for some reason it jumped off the page as though illuminated. "For Sale – 4 yr. old, chestnut, TB gelding. Track opportunity. Ready to run, jump or pleasure. Priced to sell."

Maybe it was just the timing of the ad or the fact that it was the only prospect that approached my criteria the day I began my search because in hindsight, the copy was unremarkable. Whatever the stimulus, curiosity motivated me to make the call.

The woman who answered had little information to add. "All I can tell you is he's real pretty, but we're just not horse people. I don't know what possessed my husband to buy a racehorse. I told him it was a sport for rich people, but he was sure that horse would make him one. Never did make any sense to me. But maybe this horse can win for you because like I said, he's real pretty. Fast too."

Not a convincing sales pitch, but I persevered. "What's the asking price?"

She didn't bother to disguise the hope that had crept into her voice. "Oh, the horse is a real steal. Dick's only asking $1,000. I guarantee that's far below our original investment."

"Are there any soundness issues?" I pursued.

Down the Aisle

"I don't think so, but I've only seen him twice," she apologized. "It just never was my thing. If you want more information, call Windward Farm. They're the agent for the sale."

It was a tempting proposition. The horse was priced within my allotted budget without touching the "just in case" security kicker secretly offered by Dad. Feeling a prod from my Guardian Spirit without skipping a beat, I hung up and dialed the number she had given me.

I was familiar with Windward Farm's reputation as a turnkey breeding/training facility with a top production record in the Illinois racing industry. The impressive stable was located in nearby Mundelein with acres of rolling pastures for breeding stock. It also boasted a half mile track, a private surgery and a small, oval indoor exercise track that surrounded the stalls of the horses in training.

On a rainy Tuesday morning, I was met in the foyer of the walnut paneled farm office by a curt young woman wearing a tan v-neck sweater embroidered in navy with Windward Farm. I sensed that if I had been a potential client for a pricey young prospect, a smile might have found its way across her pursed lips. She might have even offered me a seat in one of the deep, red leather wing chairs that stood against walls covered in framed photos of Windward winners. But, as my quest was for a fire sale castoff, I was only acknowledged with a brusque nod and directions to the training barn where I would find the manager.

Down the Aisle

Howard Solomon stood in the aisle, examining the front legs of a bay colt. A tattersall cap pulled partway down his forehead disguised all but a hint of an expansive bald spot. He was an overweight, middle-aged man dressed in khakis and a much larger version of the receptionist's tan Windward sweater. Despite an uneven shuffle stride as he moved around the horse, he remained in a constant state of motion, directing the large staff that kept a steady stream of horses rotating down the aisle for his inspection.

He motioned me forward with one arm while with the other he indicated a stall down the aisle to the groom standing at his side. "Leslie?" he asked without waiting for my reply. "Sorry, but we're a little pushed for time. Getting a group of colts ready to ship to the track today."

He nodded to where the groom had disappeared into a stall. "Sammy will show you the gelding. We don't normally handle this grade of horse, but the owner's a friend of a friend who got in a little too deep, so I'm helping him out. Nice enough horse, but couldn't cut it on the track. Might make a good jumper prospect though. Clean legs, no soundness issues. If you like the horse, Sammy will tack him up for you to try. Check back with me when you're done."

"Greg!" he shouted down the aisle, abruptly dismissing me as he shuffled after a groom leading a horse out of the barn. "Wrong bandages. Bring him back here!"

Down the Aisle

"So much for courting the client," I sighed, heading down the aisle toward the open stall door Howard had indicated.

Pausing in the doorway of the big box stall, I studied the striking chestnut gelding. He was racing fit, lean without an extra ounce of body fat covering cut muscles. Neck arched to the max, his small ears were pricked on high alert while he fidgeted beside the groom who held his halter.

Sammy patiently stroked the taut red neck in an attempt to relax his charge. He mumbled a soothing gibberish close to the horse's cheek to keep his attention while I slowly entered the stall.

"Don't worry, miss," he assured, without taking his eyes off Crimson Rust. "This horse won't hurt you on purpose. He ain't mean. Wants to be a good boy, but sometimes the nerves gits in his way. Just needs someone willing to put in a lot of time to build his confidence."

"Confidence," I mused, gravitating to one of my key buzz words by reaching out to the wary horse.

I gently put my hand on his withers and ran it down the slick hairs of his back. Although the horse didn't pull away, his skin twitched at my touch. Sammy's croon and my hand's steady pressure finally convinced the gelding to settle. Once I was certain he had accepted me in his space, I slowly ran my hands down each leg, exploring joints and tendons for any sign of old injuries that might indicate a potential problem. To my satisfaction, all

Down the Aisle

four legs were clean with no discernable swellings, scars or blemishes, a rarity in a horse off the track. The only obvious defect was the blatant case of jittery nerves.

I moved on to the next prerequisite on my pre-purchase check list. "Can I see him move?"

"Hey, Chris," Sammy called down the aisle. "The lady wants to see Crimson work. Grab his bridle and the jump saddle."

He winked knowingly at me. "This horse has a little extra edge, so I figure you would want a little more security up top than one of our exercise saddles."

Watching the gelding paw impatiently against the groom's restrictive hold, I wasn't about to disagree with his tack choice. I silently wondered if a seat belt might be a good option as well.

With the rain continuing to fall, Sammy opted to show the horse on the inside track that circled the stall block. It was a unique feature that allowed the horses to exercise despite the season or weather. While space restrictions limited the workout speed, the 30-foot wide track extended 200 feet down each side of the barn with an oval curve around the ends. When in use, wide barrier boards were put across each of the four entrances to the stable to prevent working horses from shying off the track into the main barn.

Despite the gelding's nervous fidgeting, Sammy easily tossed Chris up. It was lucky that the jockey managed to find the center of the saddle and stirrups in one smooth move as the trigger

Down the Aisle

of his weight ignited Crimson Rust. Finally feeling himself free of Sammy's restraining hands, the gelding was off with the explosive energy of a break from the starting gate.

Chris' fine-tuned balance followed the initial lurch, moving rhythmically with his arms and back. There seemed to be no bottom to the gelding's power, so the jockey allowed him to blow off the early energy burst before applying rein restraints to steady him.

As the gelding began to settle, I grew excited by his potential. He had an elegant, scopy canter well-suited to stride over big fences. His trot tracked up nicely with no hint of unevenness. Although I had to admit that the hot temperament was a bit of a red flag, I thought that with patience and time, I could calm the eddies that roiled through him. He would definitely be a challenge, but the athleticism exhibited was a tempting plus.

Eager for a test ride, I refused to admit to any trepidation as Sammy legged me up onto the saddle. Even though Crimson Rust had settled a bit after Chris' ride, Sammy walked the first length of the track beside me, stroking the horse to help the two of us bond.

I gave the gelding's sweaty neck a pat and smiled confidently at the groom. "I'm good to go. No worries."

"Take it slow," he advised, cautiously releasing his grip on the rein and stepping back as I urged the horse into a trot. "You're sitting on a lot of horse."

Down the Aisle

From the first strides, Crimson Rust demanded all my concentration and balance. Immediately, he bore down on the bit, increasing his trot tempo as we rounded the first turn and headed down the backside. Without urging, his trot spilled over into a canter that quickly ramped up to a gallop. I was briefly aware of a blur of curious faces peering out from the barn doorways as I rocketed around the perimeter, my mind racing with the hoof beats.

As fast as I was flying, I had an ironic sense of déjà vu from my first ride on Spellbinder, bolting across the fields with no "Whoa" button to be found. The only difference was that this time the open fields were replaced by solid barn walls that kept coming up at warp speed on a track too narrow to even consider circling to slow down.

I fought the urge to fight against the horse, willing myself to flow as calmly as possible with his movement as Chris had done. Gradually, as I stopped resisting, the pulling on my arms eased to the point where I could begin to experience the power and scope of his gait rather than just trying to hang on.

As Crimson Rust's tension eased, I was able to coax him back into a trot and ultimately a walk. We were both gasping for breath as I let the reins slide through my fingers, allowing him to flow beneath me with long, unrestricted strides. I thoughtfully stroked his neck, sensing the merging of two frustrated souls, each searching for an outlet through which to channel energies that had been stifled by circumstances beyond our control.

Down the Aisle

Rather than feeling put off by the gelding's fire, I felt stimulated by the extraordinary challenge to learn to soar with him. I knew he represented a financial gamble and physical risk for which there were no guarantees especially with such a green, hot horse. But, I also remembered that I had been successful down a similar aisle with Spellbinder. Despite the uncertainties she had presented on our first ride, the ultimate rewards had been well worth the journey.

It was a done deal not a moment too soon. Almost as quickly as the ink on my purchase check was dry, Jeff was notified that his Sears' training class was due to begin in Milwaukee at the start of the next month. By week's end, we headed north to begin hunting for a new apartment and, much to my delight, a stable.

Down the Aisle

Chapter Eight
On the Road Again

Crimson Rust carried me and my sanity through a rapid series of corporate moves. Jeff was on a faster promotional track than either of us could have imagined when he was hired. In only six years, his high speed, upwardly mobile career transferred us across Wisconsin from Milwaukee to Oshkosh to Janesville and, finally, Sheboygan. Our longest deployment was a brief two year stint, barely enough time to unpack and set up house and horsekeeping.

I realized early on that the transitory nature of Jeff's job assignments would severally affect my ability to grasp a foothold in any meaningful business or journalism career. No prospective employer was interested in investing training time in my limited window of availability. However, our married lifestyle budget necessitated both of us work to meet the monthly expenses.

My only viable professional option was to return to my first love and strongest credentials – horses. Had I remained in Chicago, my training career would have naturally evolved from established connections. However, I was soon to learn that I would

Down the Aisle

have my work cut out making inroads in the tough to crack Wisconsin horse market.

In the mid-seventies, Wisconsin beyond Milwaukee was a hinterland for the show hunter industry with a definite void of high end activities. The majority of local competitions were either breed specific or "open" shows. These multi-discipline events lopped together a wide horizontal cross-section of horses and riders usually officiated by a judge in a Stetson hat with very vertical experience. It soon became obvious that I had traversed a long way from my origins at The Academy, necessitating my aisle to take some unconventional twists as we piggy-backed across the state on Jeff's transfers.

Our first stop was Milwaukee where I boarded at Mainliner Stable, a 30 minute drive from our city apartment. Comprised of an aging wooden bank barn adjacent to a new pole building with attached indoor arena, the working area was surrounded by a quarter mile track. The stable was named in honor of its famous 26-year-old resident, Mainliner. Throughout a long career, the Standardbred stallion had trained on this track in pursuit of his 1951 victory in the Hambletonian, the first leg in Standardbred racing's Triple Crown. Celebrated for his blood lines and performance record, the high class trotter became well-known around the country as "The Horse that Made Milwaukee Famous" by beating the biggest field every assembled in the richest contest in harness racing history.

Down the Aisle

The rolling Wisconsin pastures had remained Mainliner's home throughout a successful career on the track and in the breeding shed. Upon his owner's death, a provision in the will stipulated that when the property was sold, the new owner must allow the stallion to live out his life on the farm that bore his name.

The property was eventually purchased in 1972 by Jimmy Remke, a trainer and breeder of working Appaloosas. True to the farm's deed requirements, he faithfully maintained the aging stallion in the style he had been accustomed to in his glory days. Housed in an oversized box stall with a walk-out shady paddock, he could contentedly spend his retirement surveying his kingdom.

Mainliner was definitely an ancient relic when Crimson Rust and I took up residence at his farm. With a leg cocked under his pot-bellied, brown frame, he would stand in the shade of a giant oak tree, watching the training activity like an emeritus professor. His most prominent physical feature was an extravagant roman head that he hung proudly over the fence. Jimmy told me that the racing press had nicknamed him "The Nose" for his knack of pushing it across finish lines just beyond many prettier heads to win the big races.

Jimmy Remke's professional discipline was cutting. To enhance the development of his horses, he kept a small herd of six cattle penned in the far corner of the indoor arena. Just the scent of them triggered Crimson Rust's flight instincts let alone

Down the Aisle

the sight of one of them staring him down through the rails of their pen. Mainliner's environment was certainly not conducive to settling the rattled nerves of an off-the-track Thoroughbred who suspiciously regarded his new home as a threat to his existence.

With only three other English style riders in the barn, there were scant teaching opportunities for a hunter trainer in search of a market. Before my arrival, no one in the barn had even considered jumping. There was a definite lack of training obstacles apart from the hay bales, barrels and chairs draped with indoor/outdoor carpeting that I creatively dragged out into the arena when no one else was riding. Fortunately, Milwaukee was only a brief seven month tour of duty before Sears had us on the road again.

Jeff's next assignment took us due north to Oshkosh where my best boarding option was Willow Bend Farm. The new 20 horse facility had been constructed from the deep pocket dreams of a father intent on assuring his daughters an annual place on the Wisconsin Youth Team at the Quarter Horse Congress. To this goal, Pam and Crissy Nolan were regularly upgraded to mounts that were considered politically correct from a judging viewpoint.

The "name" western trainer du jour was a regular feature at the farm. His assignment was to coach Team Nolan to the expected winning standard. The girls' job was to sit quietly in the saddle and not disrupt the work the trainer had put into their horses. With shoulders pulled back, chests pertly up, and turned-out in

Down the Aisle

the current fashion, the winning picture was framed by fixed, confident smiles.

My arrival at Willow Bend Farm coincided with Team Nolan's desire to expand their show ring horizons to include hunt seat. When the current trainer du jour's resume proved a bit thin in this discipline, John Nolan decided that my credentials fit the bill to quench the new fascination of his daughters.

An unexpected perk of teaching Team Nolan was an offer for Jeff and me to move into the green-sided farmhouse adjacent to the barn. To date, our area apartment hunting had produced very discouraging results, so we eagerly accepted the offer. Although it would require a little sweat equity, Jeff was thrilled with the economics of no rent plus a mere fifteen minute commute to his new job assignment managing the children's department at the nearby Oshkosh Sears store.

In exchange for instructing the Nolan girls and overseeing the daily business of the barn, I was also offered free board for my horse plus an opportunity to hang out my instruction shingle. I felt I was finally making some headway towards getting my training career off the ground.

Crimson Rust proved to be my best business card to break into new markets. He was a natural conversation starter with potential clients whatever their breed or discipline preference. My mastery of his fractious behavior was more convincing than words that I was up to any challenge. As soon as people watched

Down the Aisle

us work, they became intrigued by my background and how it could augment their training programs. Most potential employers operated mixed breed barns, populated by dedicated youth and amateurs who were curious, but limited in their hunter experience especially when it came to work over fences. I offered them a ready solution to enhance their client's skills while increasing the stable's revenue stream.

Crimson Rust's training was a decidedly challenging route, fraught with unpredictable twists. The hot, sensitive nature of his temperament tended to blow at the most inappropriate times with no logical trigger, sending us ricocheting around the arena at warp speed. It required a deep seat and tight hold to ride through his explosive tempests, many of which were worthy of a full page in *Ripley's Believe It or Not*. My husband presented me with a bright orange t-shirt imprinted with "Flea Power" across the chest to bluntly sum up his vision of my equine partner.

However, through patience and a bottomless reserve of intestinal fortitude, we eventually forged a partnership. I even sensed he was beginning to overcome his internal demons. Despite his insecurities, he proved to be a brilliant jumper with no fence too high or daunting. In all our years together, he never said "no" to a jump.

As soon as my mad scientist of a horse had achieved a somewhat manageable level of performance, I was itching to get back into the show ring to test his potential. However, the majority

Down the Aisle

of shows in my central Wisconsin environs were far removed from the "A" circuit hunter/jumper competitions of my Chicagoland roots. Due to Jeff's career path, I realized it might be a long time until we again lived in proximity to an area where hunters were the norm rather than the exception. With Crimson Rust ready to be tested, I didn't want to miss our moment. It was time to explore competitive alternatives.

My search hit upon the intriguing sport of eventing. Although an Olympic discipline with a tradition steeped in military origins, in the mid-seventies the competitions were few and far between. The U.S. Combined Training Association, the national governing body of the sport, had only been formed in 1959. So, it was an exciting grass roots time for intrepid devotees who wanted to share the thrill and speed of this demanding sport with their horses.

The summer I graduated from college curiosity had prompted me to volunteer as a cross-country jump judge for the inaugural horse trials to be held at the Barrington Horse Center. Assigned a log oxer, I manned my folding chair armed with a clipboard for noting clean or refused jumping efforts. Form wasn't judged, only that the pair reached the far side of the fence together. For five hours, I watched a succession of fit, eager horses gallop up, over and away. The riders attacked the course with a fearless bravado rarely witnessed in the show hunter ranks.

Down the Aisle

What attracted me most was the pure, unadulterated fun that the horses and riders seemed to share. I felt an immediate affinity for this sport that appeared to be a great day in the country, combining my favorite disciplines of cross-country riding and show jumping. The sport attracted an appealing range of characters astride an equally wide range of horses with Thoroughbreds dominating the entry roster. Competitors seemed to share a true camaraderie which was a pleasant contrast from the tight competitive cliques that peppered most hunter shows.

My bold, brilliant Crimson Rust made me feel like we were flying when he cruised around event courses.

Down the Aisle

After the final cross-country phase, I returned to the main ring to watch the stadium round held over a modified jumper course. I knew a dressage phase had begun the competition in the morning, but my jump judging duties had prevented me from watching. While I had no experience in dressage, I couldn't imagine that it would be too difficult for a rider of my experience to navigate the basic walk/trot/canter test that was interspersed by simple transitions and figures in a small 20 x 40 meter rectangular arena.

I was fired up to give the sport a try, but at the time of the Barrington event I was horseless and about to be married. However, when I found myself stranded in central Wisconsin in search of a competitive outlet, I redirected my energies toward this new, intriguing sport that had several pockets of support across the state.

It didn't take long for me to be swept up into the ranks of eventing addicts. This wild and crazy sport was the perfect fit for my wild and crazy Thoroughbred. I found it to be a pure, unadulterated thrill that I was certain my horse enjoyed as much as I did.

In the days before speeding penalties and warning cards, it was a time of joyful abandon between horse and rider. The only time penalties were for going too slow which suited my bright chestnut boy who would blow out of the start box with minimal "whoa" power until we powered across the finish line. I'm sure

Down the Aisle

many a jump judge was rocked back to hear the language of a seasoned sailor bursting from my lips as we careened over the course like a jet fighter. However, the result was always a clear round that I'm sure would have made his old track owner catch his breath in awe of the mach speeds we approached.

Armed with a new competitive outlet, I began to expand my career path. It was still a daunting challenge to develop a professional identity as I followed Jeff across Midwestern back roads through a revolving cycle of job transfers that would occur nine times in the next 24 years. With each new move, I was confronted by the frustration of starting over and convincing a whole new equine market of my worth.

Just as the skeptical new client barriers began to drop, Jeff would be rewarded by yet another promotion. Time to pack up and move again and again and again. But, despite the frequent promotions, Jeff never felt he was far enough up the corporate food chain to pull the plug and permanently put down roots in a location. So, the revolving routine continued, leaving behind newly forged friendships and training pairings that had just begun to show promise.

For many years, as I struggled to gain a foothold in ever changing new markets, Crimson Rust served as my faithful envoy. With time and patience, I discovered the buried confidence that Sammy the groom had extolled on our first meeting at Windward Farm. My flighty, off-the-track prospect evolved into a beloved

Down the Aisle

companion who made my journey through the cycle of corporate transfer uncertainties an adventure that traversed the new frontiers that had taken both of us far from our Chicagoland roots.

Down the Aisle

Chapter Nine
The School Marm

Born in 1910, Vi was a child of the Great Depression. She was raised by the strict expectations of a father who did not tolerate frivolity or wastefulness. A studious, solitary girl, she pursued a socially acceptable life path for a single woman of her era, resulting in a career as an English teacher in a rural school. The school marm never married, preferring to channel her energies toward her students and an insatiable pursuit for knowledge.

Her school district's country setting afforded Vi the cherished luxury of horseback riding for which she had harbored a passion since childhood. In her mid-twenties, she was finally able to stretch her limited resources to the max to purchase a rangy Thoroughbred on whom she devoted all her spare hours grooming and training into an obedient companion.

Impressed with the positive transformation of her mount, the local riding club where Vi boarded invited her to share her training techniques with the members. It seemed a natural fit for Vi whose disciplined classroom skills transferred easily into the

Down the Aisle

riding arena. Within a short period, she had established a weekend lesson program at the club with a growing student list.

She felt confident in her skills until the circus came to town in 1939. Spotlighted in the center ring, pranced a magnificent white stallion, mounted by an elegant, uniformed man with gold braid flowing from his epaulets. With unperceivable aids, he motivated the stallion to dance to the accompaniment of the ringside oompah band. The stallion swept sideways, skipped in the canter and pirouetted with a romantic elegance that was wildly received by the audience. Sitting forward in rapt awe, Vi's horizons were thrown open to a new style of riding that would forever change her life.

In the 1920's and '30's, the circus was a respected, popular entertainment, ranking on a par with music halls and the theater. A favorite equine act at the Ringling Brothers, Barnum and Bailey circus was a stylized offshoot of high school dressage or haute ecole. Prior to the 1960's, dressage was a little known discipline in the U.S., making the circus one of the few places where a form of the classical discipline could be witnessed.

Captivated by the intriguing unity that this discipline forged between man and horse, Vi began a quest for knowledge with the fervor of the newly impassioned. It was not an easy mission as dressage barely had a toehold in the United States in the '40's and '50's. Although competitive dressage was a centuries old discipline with deep European roots, the majority of America

Down the Aisle

was a vast dressage wasteland. The first recognized dressage show in the country was not even held until 1955. It would be 1973, 34 years after Vi first witnessed dressage, that the United States Dressage Federation was formerly chartered.

Undeterred by the challenge, Vi set out with the resilience of a hungry scholar, joining the scattered ranks of other Americans determined to learn and spread the gospel of dressage. With limited opportunity to view correct dressage or gain instruction, the result was a very seat-of-the-pants school of education for most early enthusiasts. Despite the odds, Vi not only succeeded, but excelled in her quest. By the late 1960's, she had become a champion Grand Prix competitor as well as a licensed dressage judge and sought after clinician.

After teaching school for 35 years, she retired, converting her pension into a private training stable where she could devote the remainder of her working years to the training of dressage. Tristan Oaks was a no-frills model of functionality. Fourteen box stalls lined a wide aisle that led to a meticulously groomed indoor arena. An outdoor dressage arena bordered with crabapple trees stretched beside her 2-bedroom bungalow, stained the same brown wood as the stable. Training in the outdoor was overlooked by a graveside situated just beyond "C" that was the final resting spot of her beloved Thoroughbred Grand Prix mount, Dark Warrior. Every evening at dusk she would retire with a glass of sherry to

Down the Aisle

sit on the wooden bench beside the grave marker to review the day and contemplate her friend's memory.

"Riding makes better people. They get a more humane and deeper understanding of living creatures whether it be a horse or a person" was her credo. This was just one of the many life lessons she imparted from center ring, framed by a leggy black Bouvier and a shaggy, little white mop of a dog named Rags who were her constant sidekicks.

Vi was the ultimate mistress of patience, but her world accepted no training shortcuts to attainment of the perfection that was her expected reality. No gadgets. No gimmicks. Just pure, correct riding. If students became frustrated, struggling to master a difficult dressage concept, she was quick to remind, "Patience is the greatest aspect of human nature, but it is not always displayed when learning. Now, try that again a little slower and we'll find our way forward."

I first met Vi in 1977 where she was judging at the Rocking Horse Ranch Horse Trials in the north woods of Rhinelander, Wisconsin. Her reputation preceded my nerves as I boldly trotted Crimson Rust down the centerline, crisply saluted then proceeded to disintegrate into a totally unharmonious upside-down, inside-out test. As usual, at the conclusion of the dressage phase, the scoreboard reflected my position far down in the standings going into cross-country.

Down the Aisle

For the life of me, I had never been able to soothe Crimson Rust's explosive temperament to achieve the discipline required by the four minute training level dressage test that set the stage for the remaining two phases of the event. The little white box of the dressage arena had become our nemesis. Tests that began with positive resolve in the warm-up rapidly deteriorated into a dissonant jumble once the competition ring was entered. As our ride progressed, my horse's periscope would go up, his back hollow out and the tempo increase to that of a crazed hamster on a wheel. Ask him to complete an obedient dressage test on the bit and his response was always, "Impossible. No way, no how, no deal!"

However, luck was on our side in the 1970's as the horses that excelled in dressage ring confidence usually seemed to fall by the wayside when it came to the courage demanded by the cross-country course. Despite Crimson Rust's erratic dressage performances, he always managed to jump his way into the ribbons through faultless performances in the two jumping phases.

Although Crimson Rust couldn't navigate the little white box, he never would have hesitated to jump the moon if I had pointed him at it. I envisioned there could be no stopping us if only we could reverse our fortunes in the dressage ring. How nice it would be to top the leader board after dressage rather than playing catch up from middle of the pack.

Down the Aisle

Enough was enough. I knew I needed serious help. However, despite my quest for enlightenment, there was a total void of qualified dressage instruction within hours of my current home base. Reading whatever dressage books and articles I could get my hands on had been my sole education to this point. While it had provided some thought provoking guidelines, it could only offer generic suggestions to my horse's specific problems which were a far cry from the first-hand assistance I needed.

The event at Rocking Horse Ranch provided an unexpected learning opportunity. I discovered that if I positioned myself against the rail to spectate just a few paces behind the judge's box, I could actually hear most of Vi's commentary. As the tests progressed, her clear, slightly shrill voice dictated comments and scores to the scribe who sat beside her marking the test sheets. No one seemed to complain about my location, so I spent the remainder of the morning within earshot, carefully absorbing her comments against what my eye observed in the ring.

At the conclusion of each test, Vi usually added a brief training tip to address the most obvious problem. In those few hours, her comments opened my eyes to a whole new understanding and way to view dressage. I was certain that this woman possessed the key that could overcome the only eventing hurdle that Crimson Rust couldn't clear. I knew I had to speak with her.

Down the Aisle

There wasn't an opportunity until the end of the competition when she was waiting for her ride to the airport. I thought I had a good speech prepared to present my case to this revered professional until I found myself locked into the no nonsense gaze of her steady gray eyes. They peered at me so intensely that in a moment, my professionalism dissolved, leaving me exposed as the babbling dressage neophyte that I was.

To her credit, Vi seemed more amused than put off by my stammering as I poured out my frustrations over my horse's behavior in the dressage ring. She patiently heard me out and then nodded thoughtfully before offering, "I agree. You have a serious training problem for which there are no quick fixes. However, if you are willing to invest the time to learn correctly, then you should come to Tristan Oaks with your horse to study."

With Vi there was never any fanfare or posturing. It was bluntly what it was. "As you have found, no one can learn this sport on their own. Now, I believe I have a training stall open for 2 weeks in mid-October. Here is my card. Think it over. If you are truly serious, give me a call."

It didn't seem to matter to her that the quality of my ride had been insufficient or that I lacked a resume of dressage accomplishments or even the promise of one. Perhaps she was willing to take me on in an attempt to cure one of the above-the-bit masses who offended so many judges sitting at "C". Or, perhaps she just felt sympathy for an enthusiastic competitor who just

Down the Aisle

didn't get it, but wanted to. Or, maybe, just maybe she saw a glimmer of promise in my sincerity to correct my errors before I wavered irretrievably from the path of tradition. Whatever her reason, I didn't waste time second-guessing. I signed on for those October weeks before she had the good sense to change her mind and fill them with a more accomplished protégé.

Thus, I joined the ranks of countless other aspiring Vi devotees, making the first of many 10 hour, semi-annual pilgrimages to what my husband came to refer to as Mecca. Remarkably, the portal to classical knowledge had been generously thrown open by the school marm who would become the architect of the foundation of my dressage career. All I had to do was ride through the threshold she so generously held open to begin a journey that would traverse the rest of my life.

Down the Aisle

*I was eager to absorb all that Vi
so generously offered to teach.*

Chapter Ten
Full Cry Farm

As a young girl, Dad and I hatched a secret scheme to run away to sunny California where I would have a stable near the beach filled with sleek horses. Dad, on the other hand, would fulfill his private passion of an air strip behind the barn fronted by a hanger housing a bright red Piper Cub named "The Balderdash." While Dad enjoyed playing along with the fantasy to humor my imagination, to me it was always a reality to be achieved.

When I first shared my farm dream with Jeff, he understandably balked. Being a non-mechanical, guitar-playing, suburban golfing kind of guy, he found my proposal of a backyard working stable overwhelming. While he had always been a supportive boyfriend and now husband, his role in the barn up until this point had been to hold my jacket at a show or applaud a clear round. He had never felt particularly comfortable around horses, but had unfailingly encouraged my activities. I think he always thought my passion would be appeased with the purchase of Crimson Rust and the opportunity to find fulfillment teaching

Down the Aisle

lessons in a public stable. However, that was before he was privy to my grand plan.

But with time and a genuine sympathy for our frequent transfer predicament, he slowly began to get on board with my logic. Once the stage was finally set, I plied him with a romantic dinner of beef stroganoff and a fine cabernet to close the deal. My most convincing appeal was to his wallet. I focused my argument on the rational economy of owning our own barn rather than paying board to someone else to care for my horses not to mention the commissions off the lessons I taught.

He paused in mid drink. "Horses? But, you just have Crimson Rust. How much room could you possibly need?"

"If I had my own barn I could use the extra space for some green investment prospects," I reasoned, again relying on financial logic to sell the argument. "Once they're trained, I can turn them over for a profit. Ultimately, our farm would not just cut down on expenses; it could actually make us money."

Before he could voice an opinion, I casually refilled his wine glass for the third time and slid a legal pad scribbled with careful calculations across the table. My plan as outlined was to begin modestly with Crimson Rust, a sale horse plus several boarders to help defray the overhead costs. With only a limited number of horses to care for, I assured him that I could personally handle the labor. Once the business was up and running, I could afford to hire part-time help to lighten the work load, allowing

Down the Aisle

me to allocate more of my time to income producing activities like training and teaching. On paper, it was a failsafe plan destined to succeed in the profit column.

Worn down by my persistent arguments and the financial logic of being able to write off our farm home as a business in addition to keeping 100% of the profits generated, Jeff's conservative Scottish soul finally got on board with my grand plan. However, even as the tide began to turn in my favor, I was careful to downplay the fact that 100% of the profits also meant 100% of the risk plus 100% of some very hard physical labor. There were just some aspects of the plan best to reveal only on a need to know basis.

For the next few years, my dream became our joint goal as we scrimped and saved through three ensuing transfers. Crimson Rust's board expenses and my teaching commissions that lined the pockets of other barn owners became easier to accept, knowing that my opportunity was coming. By the time move number four was announced in 1979, our savings account was finally fat enough to farm shop.

Sheboygan, Wisconsin, located on the northwestern shore of Lake Michigan, was a far cry from my childhood vision of sun-drenched California. The most remote of any of our transfers to date, the only major industry in the farm-based economy was the Kohler Company, maker of toilets, tubs and bathroom fixtures. The nearest cultural center was Milwaukee, a two-hour-drive

Down the Aisle

south. But, despite landing in the sticks, the expectation of finally purchasing my own farm brightened the prospects of the dreary location.

We were transferred in late January during one of the snowiest winters on record. Loaded in the real estate agent's Chevy Suburban, we crept down icy roads to view the limited prospects that were in our price range and Jeff's work commuting perimeter. Frigid, persistent winds off Lake Michigan had drifted snow to the top of most fence lines, making it impossible to adequately see the properties from the road let alone approximate the lay of the land. The bitter, damp cold was unrelenting freezing fingers, whipping under jackets and through many of the window casings on the old farmhouses we inspected.

Even for a dream as impassioned as mine, the frozen environment made it a daunting task to keep warm let alone imagine opening a new training business. Boarding horses, cleaning stalls, early morning feedings, even exercising horses in that toe numbing terrain was a formidable thought. How could I possibly contemplate setting up my fledgling business in this icebound Wisconsin version of Outer Mongolia?

Despite the arduous conditions, I was unwilling to delay the realization of my dream until the next move as who knew how our circumstances might change in the future? I had waited too long to let a little cold deter me from achieving my goal when I was so close.

Down the Aisle

We finally settled on an 80-year-old, two-story yellow clapboard farmhouse with a matching six stall barn on 10 acres. Originally the homestead of a local patriarch, the property was still known in the community before and after our purchase as the Scharenbroch farm even though the last family member had moved away ten years earlier. Flanked by rolling corn fields and dairy pastures, the nearest grocery and shopping center was 25 minutes away as the crow flies. Despite the drawbacks, the property was loaded with potential on a pretty setting backed by hard wood forests and the rolling Kettle Moraine landscape. It contained all the necessary elements for my business without exceeding our budget, an important fact to keep front and center as we inspected our potential purchase.

While the aging house had lots of external charm and appeared structurally sound, it definitely came with its share of internal problems. The second story lacked direct access to the furnace, relying on temperamental space heaters to cut the winter chill. The three upstairs bedrooms could only be accessed by a steep, narrow staircase not suited for the infirm of step. All of the bedrooms were void of closets. The current owners utilized an odd configuration of free standing retail racks against a back bedroom wall for their clothes storage. Although the seller had four children, the house only had one small bathroom that was located on the first floor. The cold drafts that flooded through the house were barely blocked by old, single paned windows covered

Down the Aisle

with heavy, lined brown drapes in every room including the kitchen.

The original entrance had long ago been transformed into a glassed-in sun room without an outside access door, leaving the only entrance to the home through the kitchen. Not a big issue for me since horse people traditionally used the back door, but at this point Jeff was beginning to wear the dazed expression of a deer caught in headlights.

The house's limitations were minimal compared to the interior condition of the barn. It was picture perfect from the outside, framed by a wide porch and big stall windows. However, swinging open the double dutch doors revealed a gutted structure barely recognizable as a stable. The current owners had torn out the original six box stalls, reconfiguring the barn to house a free ranging assortment of pigs and chickens whose feces adhered to every wall and surface.

Our shiny new mortgage entitled us to the daunting task of putting my humpty dumpty stable back together again not to mention sanitizing the stench from the sty to make it horse worthy. Despite the sensory overload, for the first time my own personal aisle was becoming a reality beneath the matted straw and spoiled feed that we shoveled off the floor. With each revealed foot of clean concrete, the aisle and my future prospects broadened.

Although Jeff worked by my side with minimal complaints, his enthusiasm rapidly paled as we applied a major

Down the Aisle

dose of elbow grease to scrub, nail and paint my dream into reality. "I supposed we need to name this nightmare to make it official," he wearily proposed as the stalls began to take shape. "Old McDonald's farm doesn't seem right although I've certainly felt that way since we bought it."

For 13 years, since our senior year in high school, Jeff had been my loyal supporter if not always in body at least in spirit. But now, for a brief moment, he frowned as he looked away. I should have noticed, but I was so head-over-heels relishing the reality of my grand plan that I didn't recognize the first tiny chip in his devotion to me had just flaked away.

Instead of hugging him back into our joint dream of first home ownership, I unwittingly kept my focus on the stall I was scrapping even though I knew a farm had never been the goal at the end of his rainbow. And so, the moment passed with each of us unknowingly taking a step back from two convergent visions that had slowly begun to pull apart.

I closed my eyes, visualizing all that I knew the stable could one day be. "Full Cry Farm. That's the name I picked 15 years ago, but I never told anyone just in case it would jinx the dream."

Jeff looked puzzled. "But what does the name mean?"

"It's a fox hunting term, " I explained, momentarily surprised that after so many years of horse industry exposure he hadn't picked up a working knowledge of the terminology through

Down the Aisle

osmosis. "When the hounds are on a run in full tongue after a fox it's called full cry. I've always loved hunting and it's a positive, forward sounding name. So, unless you feel strongly about another name, that's what I'd like to call the farm."

Jeff thoughtfully closed the lid on his paint can. "If it makes business sense to you and your clients, it's okay with me. So, I guess Full Cry Farm it is. There's a store in the mall that makes signs. I think they can design whatever you have in mind. I'm whipped and need a break, so I think I'll go up to the house and give them a call. I'll let you know what I find out."

And he was gone, leaving me to paint the last stall wall while visions of Full Cry Farm danced in my head. The yellow farm on County Road X was the first site of a succession of seven Full Cry Farm signs that were to be erected at the end of our driveway in four states. Throughout the years, I never considered changing the name even though my profession gradually altered from hunters to eventers and ultimately dressage which bore absolutely no connection to the hunt field. However, the continuity of the farm name gave my vision a sense of permanence in the disruptive unpredictability of Jeff's promotions with Sears that were to transfer us across the Midwest over the next 14 years.

Down the Aisle

The official Full Cry Farm sign was re-erected with each Sears' transfer.

Down the Aisle

Chapter Eleven
Murphy's Law

Three months into the establishment of Full Cry Farm, I unwittingly had a critical run in with *Murphy's Law* which, as the saying goes, "whatever can go wrong, will go wrong, and at the worst possible time." Experience has proven a direct correlation between stable ownership and this time worn prophesy. No amount of good faith, wishing on stars or talismans buried outside the barn door can indefinitely forestall the inevitable if it is meant to happen. The only unknown in the equation is who, what, where, when and how bad.

Despite the many bumps and bruises of new home ownership, the purchase of Full Cry Farm was the pinnacle of my current run of good luck. I was on top of the world, feeling invincible as I leaned on the white board fence surrounding my kingdom. Certainly it was still a work in progress, but for the first time since graduating from college I felt in control of my destiny, doing exactly what I had dreamed of for so many years.

The icing on the cake was a recently signed contract for the construction of an indoor arena. Although small, it was as large as our very thinly stretched budget could accommodate. One of Jeff's employees had recommended a local barn builder who was a cost efficient alternative to the big commercial companies, coming in 25% lower than comparable estimates. Joe Sims had passed our litmus test with a good rating from the Better Business Bureau, two referrals from happy customers and a firm, reassuring handshake. With 40% down, we were fixed on his schedule with construction to begin April 1.

I kicked my fledgling business into high gear so I could begin to contribute my share of our debt load which had ballooned into what felt like a challenge for bragging rights with the federal deficit. For the first three months, I actively promoted the business throughout the area horse community including ads in the *Wisconsin Horsemen's News* as well as joining the local chapter of the Wisconsin State Horse Council. Initially, I felt like my hunter-based business was swimming upstream against the tide of trail riders and reiners who populated the Sheboygan area, but eventually my efforts began to pay off with a string of lesson inquiries. The next challenge was to turn casual interest into profit.

Just as I was beginning to make some headway, I received a phone call from Howard Solomen of Windward Farm. I had given him a heads up that I might be looking for a green prospect once we were settled. Although the timing of his call was a bit premature especially considering the state of our finances, Howard

Down the Aisle

insisted that this was a unique, must-see prospect that fit all my requirements.

Unable to resist temptation, I headed down to Chicago with Jeff in tow as Devil's advocate. Despite my best intentions to remain detached, it was a done deal as soon as the groom walked the strapping liver chestnut colt toward us. Distinctively marked with two high white socks on the left, he had a big, very un-Thoroughbred head with a wide blaze. Although extremely handsome, his heavy bone was more reminiscent of an Irish field hunter than the lean, racing speedsters produced by Windward.

I had to laugh when Harold told me his name. "Turkey Jackson. When he was foaled, the breeding farm manager named him Jackson. But, when we brought him in from the fields to break, the jock that I put on him said he was the biggest turkey that he'd ever sat on, so the name stuck."

Noticing my quizzical stare, Harold gave the three-year-old's neck a firm pat. "No, he's not bred for our racing program. His dam's one of the farm's Quarter Horse mares that we use to nurse orphaned Thoroughbreds. Normally her foals aren't much, but this fellow's pretty well put together. Looks like he's got some jump with those hindquarters."

I had to agree that the gelding's conformation promised potential. Standing a solid 17 hands, his impressive appearance was certain to attract the attention of judges or potential buyers.

Down the Aisle

He stood quietly while I examined him regarding me with a kind, full eye.

"Nice as he is," Howard continued, "he's of no use to us since we can't race him. We don't have the capacity to train these crossbreds, so I can make you a really good deal to move him off the farm. When I knew you were coming, we tossed a saddle on and put a few rides into him to let you get a taste for his potential."

The test ride was a rousing success although it took a bit of adjustment wrapping my legs around a horse that was at least a hand taller and half again as wide as Crimson Rust. For a barely green broke youngster, he was fairly responsive and focused despite the distractions of Windward Farm's bustling training activities. The colt exhibited an active walk, energetic trot and a rolling canter which although barely navigable promised ground-covering power. The only thing I wanted to change was the outlandish name which I abbreviated to T.J. as soon as I heard it. Jeff, on the other hand, insisted the original was a classic and refused to call him anything but Turkey Jackson.

Good to his word, Howard made me an offer I couldn't refuse. Even Jeff grudgingly agreed it seemed to be a good investment for my new business. Two weeks after a clean pre-purchase exam, my sale horse prospect arrived at Full Cry Farm. But unbeknownst to me, T.J.'s invisible trailering companion was the infamous Murphy bearing the full weight of his law as the ramp dropped in our stable yard.

Down the Aisle

Jeff volunteered to stand shotgun at T.J.'s head while I mounted for our inaugural ride. Although I longed for the security of the indoor arena walls that were still a month away, I rationalized the pasture fence would provide the necessary guidance for my new youngster. Carefully, I put my foot in the stirrup and slowly pulled myself up the colt's left side, cooing and sweet talking while Jeff patted his neck.

At my weight, T.J. began to swell, trembling slightly beneath the tack. In hindsight, I should have acknowledged the colt's well telegraphed threat. But, I was too blinded by the prospect of riding my bright new acquisition on my brand new farm to heed the obvious warning signs.

Before either Jeff or I could react to the detonator we had triggered ... WHAM! I experienced the full force explosion of an equine atom bomb. Head thrown up, T.J. bolted so fast to the right that he knocked Jeff flat on his back. I found myself hurtling helplessly across the pasture clinging like a monkey to the left side of the saddle and the reins which had absolutely no affect on the bit.

"To mount or not to mount," raced through my head as we catapulted into a higher gear. The unknown factor of how the crisis might escalate if I were I to swing my right leg over the saddle surmounted the fear of letting go even though I knew I would hit the ground at warp speed. At least in the second option,

Down the Aisle

I might have some control over my fate which I knew was about to be very painful no matter what my decision.

I may have had the choice of disengagement, but my style left a lot to be desired. The jolt of the spastic crash landing twisted my lower left leg 180-degrees at the knee. Even with the wind knocked out of me, the pain was instantly excruciating. It didn't take the emergency room x-rays to confirm that I had fractured the inside top of my tibia extending into my knee.

The doctor's verdict was a wilting setback for my blossoming business. His sentence was eight weeks in a non-weight bearing, full leg cast followed by another six weeks in a soft brace with absolutely no riding for at least four months. No way, no how, no exceptions. One minute my dreams had been within my grasp and then in the bolt of a green horse, they were tumbling away in a rush of unpaid bills and unmet obligations.

My rehab sentence seemed an eternity especially considering the mounting pressures of a new mortgage, farm repairs, arena loan and the purchase of T.J., not to mention the basic necessities of food and fuel. I think the burden was even greater on Jeff, who in addition to the demands of his new assignment at Sears had to shoulder all the manual farm responsibilities that were supposed to have been mine.

To add even more stress to Jeff's plight, my mother decided to move in while I was bedridden to be certain I received proper nursing care. After two weeks with her at the helm of the house,

Down the Aisle

I don't know if Jeff was more wary of the colt's physical demands or the psychological ones of his mother-in-law. But to his credit, for keeping his patience as well as his tongue, he was definitely guaranteed sainthood by the time my mother headed home to Chicago.

After all we had been through in the brief span of Full Cry Farm's existence, you would think we were due a respite. However, Murphy's Law was working overtime a mere three weeks after my discharge from the hospital as Jeff stood sorrowfully at the foot of my bed. He shuffled uneasily from one foot to the other, trying to find the right words. Despite my pain killer induced haze, I knew it was bad news.

"Les, I hate to tell you this, but we've got a serious problem," he began slowly, but soon the crisis du jour was overflowing the room. "I got a call from the local District Attorney yesterday. He told me that our barn builder has been operating an elaborate ponzi scheme for quite a few years that just recently came to light. It appears that our deposit money along with several other folks is lost. The county is pressing charges. They want us to join eight other defendants in a class action suit."

I listened in abject horror as Jeff described that Joe Sims had undercut his competition by wide margins in order to corner the local barn building market. To meet his lowball contract quotes, he had drawn money from future projects to cover current expenses. In the end, he had fallen too far behind to legally rectify

Down the Aisle

the problem. His solution had been to sell additional contracts from which he could borrow to increase his cash flow to stay afloat. Unfortunately, we had come along at the tail end of his scheme when the wheels were coming off the wagon and there was no hope of him fulfilling our contract, leaving us with a committed bank loan for a non-existent arena.

The D.A. didn't hold out much hope of a return of our down payment, but he assured us the class action suit was our only recourse. We agreed to sign on with the other eight defrauded parties, but before we could receive any legal satisfaction, Murphy's Law struck one more time in a headline in the Sheboygan newspaper which read, "Barn Builder Commits Suicide". The grisly story detailed how Joe Sims, local husband, father and contractor had taken his life, unable to withstand the pressure of recent investigations by the D.A. into his business practices.

We absorbed the news with a conflicting mixture of anger, sympathy and frustration that drained us to the bottom of our financial and emotional reserves. It was definitely time to dig deep for a new route forward down the aisle if the farm was going to avoid falling by the wayside like so many other horsemen's dreams that couldn't surmount adversity.

I had no option but to face the decision to sell the one valuable asset I possessed in order to raise the much needed capital to keep the farm afloat. The thought of parting with Crimson Rust

Down the Aisle

was heart wrenching, but I couldn't be selfish with our financial future on the line due to the consequences of my dream and physical predicament. Jeff had held up his end of the bargain, so hard as it was I had to step up and make the professional decision. T.J. was a rough work in progress with a very long way to go before his value increased to warrant a return on my investment. However, Crimson Rust was at the peak of his ability, representing an option to return us to financial stability.

One of my new students had been totally enamored with him from first sight. Julie was a competent rider filled with desire who just needed polish. Since I was ground bound, I suggested she try a few lessons on Crimson Rust to experience a schooled horse. The chemistry was perfect which fueled Julie's fire to own him.

We worked out an arrangement that satisfied everyone's needs. Julie was to stay on as a boarder so I could give her daily help with Crimson Rust. Although by this time he had a well-educated control panel, its successful use was still a bit twitchy. In exchange for a deep discount on board, Julie agreed to take over some of the barn chores to lighten Jeff's load while I was laid up. She also offered her experience as a replacement for Jeff's uneasiness in handling T.J. who had become aware of his size and strength in my absence.

For the first time in two months, some of the tension released from my shoulders. But, while I had stopped the freefall,

Down the Aisle

I knew the fix was only temporary unless I could rectify the farm's finances going forward. I had never truly realized the constant financial drain of owning a stable. Until we purchased the farm, my career had been spent entirely on the client side of the equation, only concerned with costs directly relating to my horse. Now as a farm owner, I was staggered by the constant monetary drain from feed to bedding to insurance not to mention incidentals like light bulbs and trash bags. It was definitely a facts of life education with no sugar coating.

While the profit from Crimson Rust's sale was a welcome bandaid, our financial wounds were far too deep for this one sale to permanently heal. Although I was able to teach a few lessons propped up on my crutches, financially it didn't come close to making ends meet. There seemed no option but for me to find a desk job until I was physically able to generate sufficient farm income.

As the infamous stripper, Gypsy Rose Lee professed, "You gotta have a gimmick". Never had an expression rang truer. I knew if I were to have any hope of keeping my new stable aisle open, I would have to find a gimmick that would turn into bottom line profit. Fortunately, a promising gimmick revealed itself the next month in the form of a help wanted ad in the local paper for a media buyer position at a local advertising agency.

MGI had been formed by three executives from the outboard marine industry. Fed up with corporate pressures, they

Down the Aisle

had bundled their finances and expertise to open a firm specializing in outdoor sporting pursuits. Located two blocks from the marina in the little burg of Cleveland, Wisconsin, they built an office and a client list that afforded them the luxury of boating, skiing and snowmobiling in the name of work.

I hobbled in for my interview on crutches and one college marketing class. However, based upon the company's remote location, I must have had a deeper resume than the other applicants as I was soon offered a desk topped by a stack of outdoor sporting magazines to research. Only ten minutes from my farm, it was a convenient arrangement with a regular paycheck. Since I could still build my farm business by teaching lessons in the evening and on weekends, I stayed on at the firm for a year as Jeff and I worked our way back to solvency.

Not only did the boys at MGI know the marine industry, they had a real flair for trade show production, managing several major sporting and fishing events in Chicago and Milwaukee. My job was expanded to support these activities, giving me a very diverse education in the promotion industry. As I worked the floor of a large boat show in Chicago, I considered the possibilities of translating this sort of event to the horse industry. While some major horse shows offered retail exhibits, they focused primarily on the needs of competitors in a very vertical venue.

I visualized an all-breed expo sans competition. Similar to the sporting trade shows, retail displays and seminars would

Down the Aisle

be offered. In addition, breed associations and stallion owners could demonstrate their horse's talents to a diverse audience showcased in a big arena with a musical background. The draw would be unlimited bragging rights for the horse owners while providing an entertaining weekend for the spectators.

I sensed that I had finally hit upon a true profit making gimmick. Now, I just had to sell the idea to someone with pockets deep enough to fund the start up. I pitched the concept to my boss at MGI who was always open to the potential of new projects as long as he could smell money. Although he was unfamiliar with the horse industry, my time at the firm had convinced him of my expertise. I made sure to sufficiently stroke his ego and wallet with the suggestion that MGI could be the first to tap into this lucrative market on a whole new promotional level.

While he weighed the merits, I approached the Wisconsin State Horse Council who I knew had been considering an industry promotional weekend for years. While they lacked the finances to pull it off, they were a necessary cog in the plan. Their cross-industry affiliations would lend credibility to the fledgling event as the premise was pitched to vendors and horse exhibitors.

I carefully worked both prospective and necessary partners with my own brand of shuttle diplomacy until an agreement was reached. MGI was to be the primary partner, supplying start-up funds for artwork, advertising and facility rental. The Horse Council would be responsible for providing a large, all volunteer

Down the Aisle

labor force to work the show. Once MGI's up front expenditures were repaid including staff salaries, they would give the Horse Council 25% of the net receipts.

Both parties reached an agreement for the first Midwest Horse Fair to be held April 26-27, 1980 at the Dane County Expo Center in Madison, Wisconsin. My boss made it very clear that the success or failure of my "horsy event" as he called it rested solely on my shoulders. He named me Managing Director, charged with organizing the event, selling space and ultimately running all on-site activities. I even dragged Jeff into the plan, volunteering his radio announcer expertise to become the voice of the event.

It was a huge, creative challenge with new rules of engagement to be learned and revamped every day, but somehow we pulled it off. On a sunny Saturday in mid-April, the gates at the Expo Center opened to a crush of traffic that rapidly filled the parking lots to overflowing. I knew we were a hit when a State Trooper appeared in the show office complaining that our event had caused a major mile long back-up on the interstate at the Expo Center exit. He demanded to know why we hadn't informed the proper officials of the traffic our event would generate. But how could I inform anyone about what I could never have imagined in my wildest dreams?

In a twist of fate, the same time that the Midwest Horse Fair was taking off, the outdoor recreation industry was falling into recession, necessitating much belt tightening at MGI. Since I

Down the Aisle

was the last hired, I was the first staff member to be let go. Although my boss had been impressed with my efforts on the Horse Fair, the bottom line financial results were less than he had hoped. Considering that the state of MGI's core business would require maximum attention to remain afloat, he only wanted to stay invested in activities that he understood. Since going forward I wouldn't be on staff to interpret the horse industry, he wasn't interested in continuing the event.

In lieu of severance, he offered to sell me the name and rights to the Horse Fair for just the firm's artwork investment in the logo. For a mere $989.00, the event that I had developed could be mine. Realizing the freedom that this opportunity offered, I didn't skip a beat. I borrowed $1,500.00 from my parents to purchase the event and hired an attorney to set-up a corporation called On Course Promotions, Inc. that would be the corporate umbrella for the Midwest Horse Fair and future new Horse Fairs that I hoped to develop in other states.

As the ink on the contract dried, I sensed that Murphy's tentacles had finally released their grasp on my life. The Midwest Horse Fair had certainly taken my aisle along an unexpected path. The greatest perk of my new business was that it was totally portable. No matter where or when Jeff was transferred, I could continue to produce the event from a home office in any location. All I needed in those pre-computer days was my trusty Smith Corona, a phone line, copy machine and an overabundance of

Down the Aisle

self-discipline. In the years to come as the event grew and flourished, it was to guarantee the financial independence that would make my aisle as long and as wide as my dreams could imagine.

Chapter Twelve
The Warmblood Revolution

In my youth, Thoroughbreds ruled the day. They were the undisputed principal presence in traditional English style American equestrian sports whether it be hunters, jumpers, dressage or eventers. Morphing from racetrack careers, their classic outline and sweeping strides dominated competition arenas across the country. Secure in their domain, they failed to notice the European juggernaut headed west in a tidal wave that would forever alter the way riders, judges and spectators viewed movement in equestrian sport.

The 20th century Warmblood evolved from 19th century working horse roots on European farms and military fields. They were bred for substance, character and power to coexist sensibly with their human partners. Named for the countries and regions from which the various studbooks originated, the breeds initially exhibited distinct characteristics reflecting the specific goals of their registry. However, gradually the differences began to blur as stallions with desirable traits were jointly approved by neighboring registries to enhance gene pools. As the bloodlines began to mix,

Down the Aisle

many of the top European horses began to display a more generic appearance.

Warmbloods had long dominated the European performance scene, winning the bulk of Olympic and international medals. However, in America in the 1970's, the big moving, bulkier breeds were few and far between. Many of the early import inroads were made by World War II European refugees who settled in the U.S. or Canada. They brought with them their equine heritage and beloved bloodlines to make a fresh start in their new countries.

The early equine immigrants that trotted onto our shores bore faint resemblance to today's svelte modern types. Roman heads and thick bodies carried on stocky legs were the norm. Compared to our firecracker Thoroughbreds, the Warmbloods often appeared to lumber lethargically. But, if a rider had the skill to turn on their engines, watch out! With the right aids, incredibly suspended gaits seemed to generate from a power source that differed greatly from the flighty Thoroughbreds who appeared ground bound by comparison.

Pockets of Warmblood breeding began to spring up along both coasts as well as trickle down from the Canadian border. The first landing wave was primarily Trakehners with Holsteiners and Hannoverians close behind. The Thoroughbred community was caught off guard as the European invasion slowly spread across the country. Once the unchallenged equine Lords of

Down the Aisle

America, hoof to hoof Thoroughbreds were ultimately to prove no competitive match for Europe's Lords of the Ring.

The first Warmblood beachhead was the jumper arena where their powerhouse athleticism quickly left the Thoroughbreds eating dust at the tail end of victory gallops. The dressage community was quick to catch the wave with demand for the big moving breeds far exceeding stateside supply. The hunter world took a bit longer for the perception of the judges to transition from the Thoroughbred's traditional daisy cutter gaits. But with time, even the old hunter traditions collapsed beneath the Warmblood onslaught.

Eager to raise competitive levels to catch up with their European counterparts, Americans boarded eastbound planes. They began to frequent breed sales and training barns, importing a steady supply of quality Warmbloods to stoke the American pipeline. The European breed associations were quick to smell the money trail, following their horses westward to set up North American satellite branches of their registries to control the quality as well as the cash flow of their long established brands.

While the Warmbloods were moving west, Jeff's next job transfer moved us east to Ft. Wayne, Indiana. It was difficult to leave the friends and sweat equity we had built in the little farm that had been the realization of years of dreaming. However, I honored my agreement to support Jeff's transfers while he kept his word to help me set up Full Cry Farm #2 in our new location.

Down the Aisle

The Midwest Horse Fair had begun to generate real profits, making the move to Indiana financially and psychologically easier. With a reliable personal income stream to support future farm ventures, I finally had the financial breathing room to give my stable shingle time to attract new clients.

However, Jeff and I still faced budget restrictions necessitated by the land and facility requirements of the equine side of our domestic equation. In order to have sufficient resources for the stable, we opted for another externally charming old farmhouse with its own unique share of mechanical nightmares lurking beneath its brick two-story façade. However, the 10-acres plus newly built 5-stall barn with small attached indoor arena more than made up for the sacrifices on the house side, at least from my perspective. With everything in the barn new and ready to be used rather than painted, sanded or hammered, I had the luxury to focus on building my training business.

T.J. had made his show ring debut in Wisconsin as the Warmblood revolution was heating up. Based upon his size and type, my initial purchase plan had been to event him, but early jump training quickly revealed that he had no desire or aptitude to leave the ground. In fact, he was down right emphatic about it. However, what Crimson Rust had lacked in the dressage ring, T.J. more than made up for with a rock steady frame that caused me to redirect my focus for him toward dressage.

Down the Aisle

While T.J. proved to be a competent lower level horse, developing the lightness and suspension necessary to move up the competition levels proved challenging. It was very difficult to overcome his Quarter Horse dam's genes, evident in his low neck set and long back. Collection was a physically challenging task that felt like trying to dance ballet in clogging shoes. I was fast learning that obedience would only carry me so far toward my goal of riding Grand Prix.

I sensed I would have to climb on the Warmblood bandwagon if I wanted to break through the glass ceiling to excel in the upper levels of dressage. While the Midwest Horse Fair's continued growth made it possible for me to shop for a more suitable dressage prospect, my budget still wouldn't stretch beyond a youngster.

Although Warmbloods were beginning to intrigue many American competitors, the journalism highway was not yet stoked with a wealth of informative articles. I found the best source of information to be judges of European descent who were generous to share their firsthand experiences. I learned that Warmblood type and character within a breed tended to be consistent due to the carefully cultivated bloodlines that were identified by the first letter of the offspring's name in some registries. My season of fact finding ultimately pointed me toward Holsteiners, specifically an F-line offshoot of the foundation sire, Farnesee.

Down the Aisle

My advisors also suggested that I shop for a mare to insure the future of the investment. If my prospect was seriously injured or did not achieve her competitive potential, at least I could hope to protect or even maximize my investment through the production of a well-bred foal. Confidently armed with a wealth of sage advice, I went in search of an F-line Holsteiner filly on which to stake my Warmblood dreams.

As luck would have it, I located an established Holsteiner breeder in nearby Ann Arbor, Michigan who had several prospects within my price range, including a beautiful three-year-old filly by the stallion Fasolt who was a direct son of Farnessee. Jackpot! All my requirements in one tidy package just waiting for me three hours up the road.

The breeder hadn't exaggerated when she claimed her filly was beautiful. Finesse was drop dead gorgeous with unfaultable conformation. A very typy blood bay, she was tricked out with a well marked face and four short white socks. Still unbroken, the breeder put her on a lunge line to show off her gaits. A stunning prima donna, the filly's attitude toward discipline was quite contentious. She pulled, struck and shook her head before finally settling in to display magnificent, suspended gaits. I laughed along with her owner as we attributed the willfulness to youthful exuberance. In my experience, a little attitude was a fair trade off for that athleticism and might even serve to make her more competitive in the show ring.

Down the Aisle

Typy Finesse never failed to make an impression.

The final selling point that sealed the deal was the handsome foal grazing in a back pasture. The colt was the product of an embryo transfer from Finesse as a two-year-old. A striking miniature picture of his dam, he capered playfully around his grey surrogate. Not only was I able to witness Finesse's potential as a performance horse, but I had the unique bonus to see her reproductive potential through the colt.

Without hesitation, I ordered a prepurchase exam before some other dressage hopeful with Warmblood dreams snatched her up. However, there was an unexpected hiccup on vet check day as Finesse exhibited slight heat and lameness in her left fore which the breeder attributed to a morning romp in the field.

Perhaps that was the case or perhaps it was my Guardian Spirit warning me to take a step back. Whatever the reason, I was

Down the Aisle

too swept up in my opportunity to climb aboard the Warmblood revolution to heed the cautionary voice in my head. Determined to move forward, I waited a week for the injury to heal then revetted. This time Finesse was spot on sound, confirmed by clean x-rays and the vet's congratulatory chuckle that she certainly had a strong, independent spirit.

Nothing remained except to pay the breeder and transfer the papers. However, as I eagerly signed the check, I didn't realize that my old nemesis, Murphy, was guiding the pen. If only I had been blessed with a psychic's sixth sense. Unfortunately, I was blinded by desire as I proudly loaded my new prize in the trailer to begin what I hoped would be a formidable career.

Formidable was certainly the right description, but not in the way I had anticipated. As formal training progressed, I quickly learned that Finesse's beauty was only skin deep. Maybe she had been blessed with so much external beauty there was nothing left over for her soul. She displayed all the attributes of the little girl in the nursery rhyme who had a curl in the middle of her forehead. Because, when she was good, she was very, very good, but when she was bad she was #x#*x*! Certainly an x-rated description unsuitable for any nursery tale.

On the ground she was always an affectionate pussycat, all but purring when groomed or praised. Competing in-hand, she was undefeated, earning blues and "ooh's" from spectators and judges alike. However, if she was Dr. Jekyll in-hand, she

Down the Aisle

certainly transformed into Mrs. Hyde under saddle where she could morph from breath-stopping to just plain stopping.

She had a rapid fire ejection button with a very twitchy trigger that was quick to go off with an emphatic "NO!" without apparent cause. The result was a stiff-legged, humpback launch straight upward then sucking back all in one athletic, willful move that rarely failed to dump me in an inglorious heap. Rather than take off bucking like a normal horse to celebrate her newly won freedom, Finesse would stop near where I lay gasping for breath. As I checked for personal damages, she would turn in my direction, gazing arrogantly just slightly over my head to remind me who was truly the boss mare.

As the disappointment and physical pain that were to mark our relationship ramped up, I was forced to admit that the principal in my personal Warmblood revolution had turned traitor. Drastic outside assistance was going to be required if I were to survive the experience and get my plan back on track.

In an effort to salvage my investment, not to mention physical well-being, I loaded up my mare and headed south to Meredith Manor in West Virginia to enlist the assistance of the sagest European trainer I knew. It was the first time in my riding career I had considered handing over my reins to another trainer. Prior to this point, I had firmly believed that if I worked hard enough any result was achievable however, that was before I had met Finesse. By this point in our relationship, my bruised body

Down the Aisle

was far more painful than any hit my ego might take from outside assistance.

I knew if anyone could give Finesse the much needed attitude adjustment, it would be Bodo Hangen. Through seasons of watching him in the competition ring and clinics, I had never seen him unseated or even rumpled by any of the challenging mounts he trained to high levels of success. He had always been the epitome of disciplined execution to which horses seemed to willingly submit.

Hopes were high the morning Bodo confidently swung aboard Finesse, patting her neck as they moved off in harmony. My mare obediently trotted and cantered through basic figures, earning encouraging praise. All was copasetic until Bodo ramped up the pressure. Just as quick as you could say "Stop…hump…launch", Bodo flew off backwards, hitting the ground with a resounding thud. He lay motionless, flat out on his back in the middle of the busy arena that had gone dead still. Finesse stood quietly to his right with a hind led cocked, looking calmly past her downed victim directly at me, quietly relishing her first round knock-out.

I watched in abject horror. While personally suffering similar traumas too many times to count, I had never actually witnessed it. Now, seeing Finesse in full-blown action, I realized I had never stood a chance even if super glue had been applied to the seat of my breeches.

Down the Aisle

Bodo was very slow to rise. He opted to end the training session for a trip to the doctor to check out his back that was causing him to walk with a painful tilt. Fortunately, there was no break, but the doctor sternly grounded him for two weeks. There was nothing left for me to do but apologize profusely and head back to Ft. Wayne with my strong-willed, self-centered beauty queen, her crown and attitude still firmly centered.

Throughout my years training horses, I had always gravitated toward challenging projects whose hidden inner character glowed encouragingly through the cracks. Ultimately, I had reaped satisfying rewards through patience and love that left me eager for the next challenge. I don't think any of my past good experience with difficult horses had prepared me for Finesse who had turned out to be the proverbial bad seed in the glossy apple. Too late I realized I had put vanity before wisdom in my purchase decision that had in hindsight valued beauty over character.

Despite the certain pain that lay down the training road, I refused to give up on such an inherently talented, beautiful horse. With Bodo no longer an option to ease my journey, I decided to give it one more try, hoping above hope that the maturity that came with age would ultimately make her more receptive. Even in her worst moments, Finesse had always offered just enough promise of brilliance to keep me a believer. Besides, if she truly wasn't the horse for me, how was I ever going to find a buyer unless I could at least modify the problems?

Down the Aisle

Finesse issued her final act of defiance on the day I was determined to take a stand against her willfulness. Once and for all, I resolved to transform her belligerent "NO!" into a submissive "Yes, Mam." Armed with an extra long whip and rowled spurs for back-up, the session began amicably enough with the polite formalities of responsive horse accepting long rein stretching. Her relaxed breathing followed the beat of long, flowing strides that fell into rhythm with the Vivaldi playing over the indoor arena speakers.

It was a pleasing moment that teased with the promise of all that could be. If only I could just foster this obedience into permanence. The cooperative glimmer that marked the beginning of each ride always left me with the hope that I could make a difference, if not this ride than the next. Silly me to fall prey to blind delusions. After two years, I should have known better than to be suckered in as I once again fell victim to the same weaknesses that govern most abusive relationships. With each positive start, I would allow myself to believe that the worst was finally behind, only to be disappointed and battered midway through the ride by an unwilling partner.

This day I was determined to meet whatever she threw as she had embarrassed or dumped me in the dirt one too many times. After all, I was the pro and she was my protégé. Or so I thought until she unleashed the full fury of all she possessed.

Down the Aisle

Right on cue, as I shortened the reins, deepened my seat and asked her to engage, she unloaded. I wouldn't be exaggerating to say we were both surprised that I was still firmly seated after the second leap. That disbelief may have been the cause of her momentary hesitation which gave me an opportunity to draw upon my resources.

Determination buoyed by the newfound confidence that I was still on board would rule this day, I cranked hard with the left rein to prevent a third buck. Rather than submit, Finesse added a diabolical new twist to her repertoire. Quick as a spark, she reared, throwing herself angrily against my left leg. The force of her action combined with my demanding rein aid, threw us both off balance. Before I had the time or foresight to release the rein and kick her forward, she flipped over, crashing to the ground on top of me.

The pain was instantly excruciating. My pelvis took the full brunt of the mare's weight as I fell spread-eagled beneath her. She rolled left then right in an effort to scramble to her feet. I heard a sickening crack as I felt my pelvis tearing apart. Nausea rose above the cacophony that rang in my ears. An intense white light swelled with the pain, but failed to bring the blessed relief of passing out.

The old saying asks, "If a tree falls in the forest, does anyone hear it?" As the independent owner of a small training farm, I was that tree, rarely having the luxury of a supportive body within earshot unless I was teaching. Consequently, I now

Down the Aisle

found myself totally alone mid-arena, plastered into the sand with no prospect of help for at least an hour when my first lesson was due to trailer in.

I lay still for a long time, afraid to assess the damages. Chills began to spread over me as shock set in, raking my core with uncontrollable tremors that ramped up the pain in my pelvis. I focused on slowing my breathing, trying to relax some of the tension that gripped every fiber of my body.

Without turning my head, I was aware that Finesse had come up behind me. She curiously reached down to snuffle my hair. "Great," I moaned, feeling totally vulnerable. "She's come back to finish off her prey."

The last thing I needed was for her to paw at me. Realizing that my left fist still clenched the whip, I feebly swished it in her direction. While Finesse certainly no longer perceived me as a threat in need of an aggressive response, at least she had the decency to wander away from what she now probably considered road kill.

Bit by bit I began to test my extremities. Fingers, feet, neck all appeared functional. While my arms felt incredibly heavy, they could move and bend. Breathing was very short and difficult which probably meant ribs were involved. But, the major cause for concern centered on my pelvis. I felt like I had been split in half. The pain warned me not to try sitting, twisting or rolling.

Down the Aisle

There would definitely be no way to even drag myself across the arena to the phone in the office to call for help.

I was helpless as the scarecrow in the Wizard of Oz where the evil flying monkey in the Holsteiner mare costume had stripped me of all my stuffing and left me finished in the dirt. There was nothing to do until my student arrived, but try to remain as calm as possible and conscious to fend off future advances by Finesse who was again heading in my direction.

An eternity seemed to pass until Debbie appeared in the barn with the paramedics quick to respond to her 911 call. The rest of that day as well as the next two weeks passed in a morphine induced haze, gratefully dispensed by a hospital I.V. I had vague memories of medical staff, Jeff, my parents and assorted friends passing in and out of my room, but very few thoughts overrode the pain and drugs.

The prognosis from the doctors for total recovery wasn't encouraging. While I had been spared internal injuries, the accident had totally broken through the left side of my pelvis, causing severe nerve damage down my leg. Although my hip had not been broken, the pelvis was permanently misaligned. There was no way to know the long term extent of the injury, but depending upon how the damaged nerves healed, the doctors had serious doubts about my future as a professional rider.

As my lucid moments grew and physical therapy began to get me cautiously moving, talk turned to returning home from

Down the Aisle

the hospital. I should have been encouraged by the physical progress and the loving support of family and friends who had become fulltime cheerleaders. But, whenever I thought about my beloved barn, all I could visualize looming down the aisle was a gaping black hole, a specter of doubt that sucked in all my energy and courage to move forward.

At first I assumed it was just a cruel side effect of the morphine. But, even after the I.V. was removed, the gaping black hole remained, daily growing larger to encompass all my thoughts even though I refused to mention them aloud to anyone.

Fear. I had never before been truly frightened by my sport. Over the years I had certainly experienced my share of bruises and breaks, but up until this point I had considered them little more than painful, inconvenient speed bumps. They may have slowed me down during the healing process, but I had always bounced back with renewed vigor. Even my knee injury from T.J. had never made me hesitate to put my foot back in the stirrup. Now, for the first time, I had to admit that I felt totally overwhelmed as my overpowering love of my horses and sport came face to face with that black hole of doubt that consumed my every waking thoughts of returning to the aisle.

Down the Aisle

Chapter Thirteen
The Mighty Quin

A bright-eyed bay foal with a long white blaze nursed confidently at his dam's flank. He had no idea of her importance outside the realm of his physical needs as she gently nuzzled his hip, flicking her tail to swish away the summer flies. Tusquin's only concerns of food, sleep and nurture were lovingly met by the big mare and her owner.

The bandy-legged Dutchman was a fulltime policeman. Like many of his countrymen he had a passion for fine sport horses. He and his wife had even gone so far as to channel their energies and savings into a small farm that supported three well-bred broodmares. His "girls" were treated with family devotion to reward their production of highly marketable foals.

He had eagerly awaited the birth of this three month old colt out of his top mare, Ole Prinses. She herself was the product of his earliest breeding experiment and now represented the prime example of his growing expertise. Entering the peak of her reproductive years, the mare would ultimately earn National recognition for the production of seven winning FEI horses, one

Down the Aisle

who would go on to represent Holland in the Los Angeles Olympics.

Although the breeder and his wife doted on their foals, they were not riders with competitive aspirations. All the offspring were destined to be sold to support the hobby that they hoped would one day fund their retirement. The big mare was their top dam. Initially, her foals remained tucked away in the thick pasture behind the stone barn, growing in stature and value as rumors of Ole Prinses' latest promising offspring spread throughout the horse community. As her blue chip broodmare reputation grew across Holland and beyond, the breeder's farm became a popular port of call with trainers seeking that something special for clients.

Ole Prinses loved her job and the breeder loved her for it. An easy producer, she was bred annually to the top dressage bloodlines. Tusquin's sire was Ormand, a popular Selle Francais approved by the Dutch Warmblood studbook to produce the more refined, modern outline desired by sport horse buyers. His progeny generated media hype for their high inspection scores that resulted in increased gilders for the breeders.

While Tusquin was maturing on the little farm, a young Dutchman caught a full blown case of horse fever. Exhibiting a natural aptitude from an early age, Roelf's parents had enrolled him in lessons at the local riding club. His father was a tradesman by profession, specializing in home remodeling. While he expected his only son to follow him into the business, he humored

Down the Aisle

his child's adolescent passion by purchasing his first competition horse. When Roelf's skills began to draw attention at local shows, he was invited to study with a respected senior trainer.

It wasn't long before Roelf became impatient with his ageing mentor whose focus was on slow, classical development rather than the glory of competitions and silver cups. With Roelf's ambitions focused on the highly competitive national FEI Young Riders program, he was certain he could achieve international exposure if he just had what he considered more modern training. While his current coach and horse had been good stepping stones, he felt the keys to reaching the top of the sport were a new trainer as well as a mount with greater physical horizons.

Roelf's talents were soon noticed by a dynamic up and coming trainer who was setting the competition scene on fire with controversial training techniques that were producing winning results at home and abroad. Impressed with Roelf's skill and determination, the trainer offered him a working student position.

As fate would have it, the trainer discovered Roelf and Tusquin at the same competition in Maastricht. The now seven-year-old gelding had quickly moved through the training cycle since his initial sale from the breeder's yard for a handsome profit as a highly touted three-year-old. He had been broken by a well-known dealer who specialized in starting superstar youngsters. In short order, he was profitably sold again into the hands of a competitive professional who added a little more polish then

Down the Aisle

promptly resold him to a wealthy business man whose young wife admired the gelding's sparkle and winning presence.

As a colt, Tusquin had been eager to have a job. His early handling with the breeder had been positive, reinforced by kindness and praise. However, once trailered away from the little farm, his training regime was ramped up with short cuts designed to highlight his flamboyant gaits without taking the time to build a solid base. All the investors on his training path had only focused on window dressing gimmicks that would generate profits rather than create a confident, happy horse.

In short order, the eager joy that had begun Tusquin's career was replaced by a reluctant obedience. By the time he trotted down the centerline at the Maastricht show with his frustrated blond rider angrily thumping her heels into his sides, he exhibited only a hint of the promised talent. The once supple, flowing gaits were barely evident through his locked jaw and over-flexed frame.

As the trainer watched, he remembered the early talk about the gelding's brilliant prospects that had been the dream of many tack shop conversations. Now, as he observed the rider's tight jaw set as hard as her horse's, he knew that for this woman the dream had long ago ended. Sweat streamed down her brow as the gelding lugged her ingloriously through the movements. At the end of the test, she dismounted quickly, throwing the reins to a waiting groom in disgust without a pat for the once shiny new toy that no longer worked its magic for her.

Down the Aisle

The trainer was able to see beyond the resistance created by a poor rider. He was certain the gelding's natural potential still existed below the surface, making him a good investment at the right price. Given the woman's obvious distain for her mount, now was the time to make an offer. If Tusquin could be had cheaply enough, there were definitely gilders to be made. Better yet, the trainer realized he might not even have to take any money out of his pocket if he could sell the woman the elegant chestnut he had brought to the show. While the mare's long range prospects were limited by average gaits, she was an easy ride and a pretty little diamond to complement the rings on the woman's hands. Rarely failing to succeed at the game at which he had become so proficient, the trainer left the show with extra gilders in his pocket, Tusquin in his trailer and a promising working student scheduled to start on the horse in a week.

The match was a good fit for the trainer and his protégé. Roelf was a willing sponge, eager to soak up whatever his new mentor required. His exposure to the trainer's lucrative world of expensive horseflesh and deep-pocketed clients fueled his ambitions to someday illuminate his own spotlight far beyond the limitations of his father's remodeling business. Once he'd had a taste of a world that didn't include spackle and hammering nails, he knew he could never go back. He set about convincing his father that with time he too could create and sell big ticket horses like those that had made his trainer famous.

Down the Aisle

Tusquin became Roelf's vehicle to make his name. From the beginning, the gelding represented an advancement tool rather than a partner with whom to grow. While the trainer's system worked for Roelf, for Tusquin it just represented another unhappy stop in the revolving barns he had passed through. Although he received the best in feed, stabling and maintenance, the nurturing bond that he had enjoyed as a youngster at the breeder's farm was a long forgotten memory.

The trainer's rigid system and the powerful young man's athleticism left him little option but obedience. As they began to break through Tusquin's stiffness, Roelf claimed personal credit for the evolving improvement, rather than acknowledging a team effort with the horse. Not a fighter by nature, Tusquin reconciled to his new role. He didn't love the impatient young man. He didn't love the system that withered the final remnants of his joy. But, he showed up every day and did his job because the system didn't allow for less.

Tusquin noticed other horses come and go from the training barn, guided by Roelf or the trainer into the hands of expectant buyers who loaded them into trailers in search of awards in far off towns and countries. He wondered when he too would again be handed off to a new set of unsympathetic hands and demands.

When the Prix St. Georges movements had been confirmed, the trainer deemed Tusquin ready to return to the show

Down the Aisle

ring. While his results were greatly improved, the sparkle of brilliance necessary to win the big classes was still lacking. After a season of lackluster, fault free performances that usually placed in the low ribbons, Tusquin had still failed to top the podium. The trainer decided that although the horse was consistent, he would never rise to the demanding standards of top European competitions that would result in a big return on his investment.

Always the businessman, he knew there was still a profit to be made. If not at home, he would follow the money trail westward to the hot U.S. market where demand was high and competition standards had not yet reached European prerequisites. With a good American agent consigned, all that remained was to make a sales video, organize the paperwork and book a flight to the States for the gelding.

Meanwhile, on the other side of the Atlantic, I had just been promoted from crutches to a cane as I slowly recovered from the broken pelvis. Three months after the accident, the doctors had given me a cautious albeit skeptical green light to remount and begin short walking sessions on T.J.

While riding had been put on hold for several months, I had been forced to take a sobering look at my horse future. I wondered if the dreaded black hole with its paralytic grasp on my consciousness would allow any wiggle room for moving forward. For the first time in my life, I experienced a serious loss of confidence, bordering on what I hated to admit was fear. Was

Down the Aisle

there still a place for me in the aisle that I had worked so hard to build?

When confronted by injuries in the past, desire plus youth had always made me feel invincible. However now, although not old, I was pushing 37 with quite a bit of wear on my personal tread. This accident had definitely made me face my own mortality.

It was tempting to surrender to the easy solution of my husband's advice to remain safely grounded by refocusing my energies on event promotions. As the Midwest Horse Fair had continued to grow and prosper, I had received consulting commissions to help a variety of organizations develop similar events across the country. But, I knew in my heart that I wasn't cut out to be a fulltime desk jockey no matter how creative or lucrative the project.

Jeff hadn't been shy expressing his abhorrence at going through any future horse-related accidents. "Do you realize how lucky you were? You do understand that you could have easily been paralyzed or killed. How do you think I felt seeing you so hurt in the hospital? It's just selfish to our relationship to keep testing fate with these crazy green horses."

It would have been so easy to fall in line with his logic that meant no more lump in the throat when I put my foot in the stirrup even on steady TJ. No need to marshal every fiber of resolve to override the painful ache in my pelvis every time I cautiously swung my leg over the saddle. No more racing heart when I gathered up the reins.

If my breath shortened to squeeze my chest at a school horse walk, how would I ever again be able to push the envelop to attain my goals? Despite the fear, horses were still my heart song. There had to be a way to override the pain and nerves to hear their music again.

In the past, I had taught students who had professed fear over a myriad of triggers from jumping fences to correcting balky horses. I always encouraged them with my "courage conquers all" mantra along with the tried and true wisdom of throwing their heart over any obstacle for the horse to follow. But, now stopped dead by my own fear, I wondered how it would be possible to throw my heart forward when it seemed paralyzed.

While my future was still a huge unknown, Finesse's fate had been sealed while I was in the hospital. Although a highly questionable performance prospect, her bloodlines and conformation still made her a premier broodmare candidate. I had always had a standing offer from the previous owner to buy the mare back for her breeding program if she did not work out. While it was beyond me why despite Finesse's physical beauty anyone would want to risk reproducing her she-devil character, I wasn't about to argue with the generous solution.

Once the initial cause of my fear was gratefully loaded on a trailer back to Michigan, the next hurdle was to restore my

Down the Aisle

confidence. With dear T.J. as a guide, I slowly began the process. We had come a long way since that first ill-fated ride at my Wisconsin farm. Over the years, we had learned to trust each other to the point that I now felt safe to put my physical well-being in his able hooves.

Quiet, easy walks in the indoor gradually grew into the elixir of long, cross-country hacks, soaking the sun and breeze into my hair as I rediscovered the joy that had stoked my youthful days in the saddle. Gradually, ever so gradually, I began to tip toe around the black hole.

Moving forward, I knew I wasn't ready and might never be to risk the uncertainty of another unproven youngster. My heart and very battered body were not up to the task no matter how tempting the prospect. Besides, I had come to realize that if I were ever to achieve my goal of riding Grand Prix before I was AARP eligible, I would need to elevate my education. Although well-versed over fences, as far as dressage was concerned, my personal experience was still green. Unlike hunters, in the discipline of dressage I still lacked the skill and experience to make something concrete from the unknown presented by an untrained horse. Even though I had listened, watched and read all the very best theory available, my green horses and I seemed perpetually stuck beneath the glass ceiling of Third Level.

I had gotten this far in the sport by toughing it out on my own, supplemented by trailering to distant clinics. But, without a

Down the Aisle

way to feel correct collection and upper level movements, I was stymied. Unlike Europe, American dressage at that time was still in its formative stage with very limited access to trained lesson horses especially in small Midwestern markets like Ft. Wayne where, much to my amazement, I currently represented the highest local level dressage instructor.

If I were truly to improve beyond my rut, it was time to consider purchasing a legitimate schoolmaster. After so many years of being the teacher, I realized that a little role reversal was necessary if I was ever to progress in the sport. It was time to purchase a highly trained dressage master from whom I could learn.

The perfect candidate would be a proven competitor possessed of a calm temperament to nurture my frazzled confidence. Ideally, he would be well-versed in the advanced movements of the F.E.I. so I could develop my skills to the highest level.

Although determined to move forward, it was hard to justify the expense given that Jeff's and my domestic finances had once again been battered by the recurring demands of our latest charming, albeit crumbling farm house. While my current budget fell short of the projected cost of an F.E.I. venture, my parents came to the rescue. Always uneasy over my green horse adventures, they determined to turn their fears into supportive action. Hoping a schoolmaster would prevent future hospital

Down the Aisle

forays, they offered an interest free loan, offsetting repayment until the receipts were banked from the next Midwest Horse Fair. It was all the encouragement I needed to kick my plan into action.

For the remainder of my recovery, I focused on finding the best schoolmaster I could afford. Once the word was out and the smell of new money in the air, I was barraged by agent phone calls and tempting sales videos of "must see", "not-to-be-missed", "one-of-a-kind" opportunities. With the exception of Finesse, I was used to searching for off-the-track bargains, so it was a new experience to be a courted client. While I might have been new to my price range status, I certainly wasn't new to the creative tricks of the selling game. Many of the flashy prospects came with beautiful chrome and impressive tricks-on-tape, but closer inspection often revealed slight gait hitches or clever video editing to conceal movements gone wrong.

I came across several promising "maybes", but I didn't get my first serious case of goose bumps until viewing a tape of three recently imported Dutch Warmbloods. There was an extravagant, all legs three-year-old stud colt touted to be the "Second Coming", a serious Grand Prix champion who was laughably far beyond my borrowed budget, and a solid, attractive 10-year-old bay gelding competing successfully at Prix St. Georges. While the first two horses were definitely a pleasing eyeful, it was the third horse that made me tingle.

Down the Aisle

Rather than being bitted up tightly in a double bridle, he was ridden easily in a plain snaffle by a long legged, athletic young man. Round and supple, the gelding's gaits looked like comfort personified. As the video progressed, they worked obediently through all the Prix St. Georges movements even exhibiting a positive start of piaffe and passage. No matter how many times I viewed the tape, I couldn't find a drawback. With each viewing I grew more eager to meet this intriguing bay Dutchman. Character was one of the top criterion on my shopping list; and, this guy seemed to have a ton of it. But, knowing tapes could be very deceptive, I tried to keep my hopes in check.

The selling agent was a respected trainer in Chicago with whom I had cliniced. She confirmed there had already been a lot of interest in these special horses due to arrive in her barn from quarantine the following week. She warned they would be sold on a first-come, first-served basis, so if I were interested I shouldn't delay my travel plans.

Determined to be the first to tryout the bay gelding, I reserved the earliest available showing date after his scheduled arrival in Chicago. Although my pelvis was still not sufficiently healed to be able to sit deeply enough to get a true feel, I felt I had regained enough of my skills to fairly test ride a trained horse. Besides, I felt confident that I could benefit from the trusted agent's expertise.

Down the Aisle

After a five-hour-drive to Chicago that seemed an eternity, I finally found myself in front of the stall that held the object of my imagination. Even before our official meeting I had felt intuitively drawn toward him by a force I sensed shouldn't be ignored. Why after viewing so many promising sales videos did I keep returning to this particular horse?

The agent swung open the door to reveal my first glimpse of Tusquin. I'd like to say our eyes connected across the stall and it was instant love declared on a soft nicker. But, obviously my expectations had overblown reality as the gelding barely made eye contact before shrugging us off to return to his snooze against the back wall. The trainer wasn't concerned, excusing his lack of interest to travel fatigue as she went to get the tack.

I quietly entered the stall, slowly offering an open hand in greeting. Tusquin remained motionless, accepting my touch without the reciprocity of even a slight nuzzle. Confronted by his aloof demeanor, I had to admit a bit of disappointment. My imagination had run wild since viewing his video, concocting fantasies of being championed around big time arenas by the powerful bay gelding who happily carried our partnership forward.

I quickly reminded myself that I was in the market for a serious training mentor, not a personality. I already had a pet at home in T.J. who was permanently stuck at Second Level. This time personality wasn't important as long as Tusquin had the character and ability to safely do the job required. However, once

Down the Aisle

the trainer led him from the stall and began to put him through his paces, personality seemed even less important as his gaits filled the arena from fluid half passes to straight, dynamic flying changes.

Despite my eagerness to put the accident behind and move my training forward, I had worried until this moment how my battered nerves would respond to the challenge of mounting an unknown horse. But, as I watched Tusquin's willing answer to every question the trainer asked, I felt my anxiety melting away. I realized for the first time since the accident that I couldn't wait to put my foot in the stirrup.

To my delight, he responded with total obedience even though I was quite certain some of my fumbled aids were gibberish to him. Although I was out of shape and still recovering from the accident that restricted my ability to sit deeply, Tusquin never took advantage of my weaknesses. His patience seemed bottomless as I could almost audibly hear him sigh, "Wrong answer. Come on, try again."

With the trainer's coaching and Tusquin's tolerance, I experienced the thrill of executing movements that up until that moment I had only spectated from the sidelines of clinics or shows. My only disappointment was that although Tusquin dutifully tried to answer every question, I sensed he didn't hear the same music that resonated crescendos through my every fiber with each new movement revelation.

Down the Aisle

After 30 minutes in the saddle, my confidence was bubbling out of the black hole that had held it captive since the accident. Even though it was only our first ride, I was certain that I had truly found a schoolmaster worthy of the title who could restore and elevate me to a whole new level.

Although it seemed like a quick decision for such a major purchase, I sensed that even if I tried a dozen other prospects, I would not find another who so ably built my confidence while enhancing my skills. Based upon the appointments the trainer had scheduled for other prospective buyers to test ride Tusquin, I was certain he wouldn't remain long on the market. Taking a deep breath, I sealed the deal with a pat on his neck.

Once the vetting and paperwork were completed, the agent sent us home to Ft. Wayne with the barn's traditional new horse champagne celebration. Popping the cork on a bottle of Moet, sugar cubes were splashed with the bubbly then happily fed to Tusquin while the human revelers toasted tidings of good rides to come.

It was a memorable celebration to inaugurate a relationship that was to grace my heart and stable for the next 18 years. We began as two searching souls brought together across an ocean by chance or maybe fate, the shell of a great horse who had lost confidence in humans and the shell of a rider who had lost confidence in herself.

Down the Aisle

Tusquin's past training routine had been so structured that it took many months for him to learn to enjoy life outside the arena where the freedom of pasture turnout didn't result in fenceline pacing. Gradually, I noticed a curiosity begin to shine from his bright eyes as he took a new interest in me and his surroundings.

With that fresh connection, my real dressage education began from a wonderful Dutch mentor who daily convened lessons in the arena. In me he found an eager pupil, who willingly traded my traditional role as trainer for that of student. I learned to listen to all he offered until my skills deepened to the point where I caught up to his knowledge. On that day we went forward as equals, both finally hearing the music that had marked my first ride on him.

Those memorable lessons were to benefit all the future horses that would pass down my aisle. They became the lucky beneficiaries of Tusquin's wisdom and skill that forever transformed the foundation of my riding. What an education it was to be as he ultimately guided me all the way down the center line of the Grand Prix ring. My only charge for those invaluable lessons was patient, unconditional love.

Down the Aisle

*__Tusquin's invaluable lessons guided me
all the way to Grand Prix.__*

Down the Aisle

Chapter Fourteen
My Memorable Mentor

As the old saying goes, "All roads lead to Rome." Unfortunately, that adage doesn't necessarily apply to the myriad of philosophies that have evolved over the centuries to guide the journey of dedicated horsemen in their training pursuits. While some theories are spot on, not all are compatible with logic. Although many evolved from proven classical concepts, some bubble up from new age hocus pocus.

Not all training roads result in the desired success. Not all are universally embraced. However, despite their differences, each philosophy originated from a sincere need to mold the horse's character and talents to fulfill the trainer's requirements. Dating back over 2,000 years to the first written essays on horsemanship by the ancient Greek Xenophon, man has sought the most effective methods to enhance his relationship with the horse whether for war, work, competition or pleasure.

Throughout my years in the horse industry, I was fortunate to benefit from the expertise and inspiration of many gifted instructors. My quest for knowledge led me down a variety of aisles forged by each trainer from their own hard learned studies in the aisles of their respective mentors. Each bestowed on me

Down the Aisle

their personal training philosophies in the "pass-it-on" tradition as I learned my way into the fraternity of instructors.

From the Captain's strict European traditions to Flo's pragmatic wisdom to Vi's school marm discipline to all the others whose lessons so generously filled in the blanks, I grew from their experience. Over the years, I circled countless arenas under their watchful eyes that forged the foundation of the instructor I was to become. When I finally felt confident to hang out my own professional shingle to invite students down my aisle, it was with profound gratitude for all the sage knowledge I had absorbed from my mentors.

I loved teaching from my earliest experience at age 16. In exchange for Tic-Tac's board, I was honored to be invited to become one of the Captain's Summer Camp staff. Like many before me who had come up through the ranks of his system, I taught rudimentary walk-trot-canter basics to the new pre-teen faces who rode the little red bus. From the first time I stood center ring circled by those eager, horse fever flushed faces, I was inspired.

Even when faced with the awkward fumblings of beginners, I loved the creative challenge of molding horse and rider into a cohesive partnership through words rather than physical action. To guide them successfully through what had initially seemed an insurmountable physical or psychological hurdle, was the ultimate challenge as well as reward.

Down the Aisle

My passion for teaching also became a safe haven especially in times of personal stress or loss. Whenever external pressures seemed particularly daunting, I found welcome sanctuary within the walls of the arena. Once immersed in the concentrated details of a lesson, those "real world" anxieties quickly dissolved.

None of my mentors made a more lasting impression upon me than the man I still find myself quoting in lessons decades after our first meeting. Major Anders Lindgren was the son of a Swedish cavalry officer. He was born in the 1920's into the military tradition of horsemanship as the gauntlet was passed from father to son. From early childhood, it was obvious that he had been gifted with an affinity for riding, evident from his delight the first time his father straddled him in front of his saddle.

It was a natural evolution for the boy to follow his father into the cavalry, ultimately rising to the rank of major. For the next 30 years, the military was his passion and profession. His equestrian prowess resulted in winning the Swedish National Championships in eventing and dressage as well as representing Sweden in the Olympics. Finally, in 1975, he retired from the military to pursue a civilian equestrian coaching career in Sweden, Finland, Norway and ultimately the United States.

Vi initially brought him to the attention of American dressage riders. In the summer of 1981, she invited him to coach at the 2nd annual National Trainers' Symposium that she had established at her Tristan Oaks. Twelve aspiring instructors with

Down the Aisle

horses ranging from Training to the FEI level as well as 20 auditors were privileged to be invited by Vi to participate in the week long program that in later years would evolve into the USDF Instructor Certification Program.

We came from all corners of the U.S. from California to Florida to Massachusetts and points in between, eager for the opportunity to participate in this unique learning experience that combined classical theory with practical instruction through the levels. I was honored to be selected with T.J. as one of the fortunate 12. Heading east to Michigan from our Sheboygan farm, my pride at being chosen was tempered by the uncertainty of whether or not my First Level nurse mare offspring and I would be up to this noted European master's standards.

While all of the Symposium participants were awed by the depth of the Major's credentials, none of us knew what to expect of his teaching style. Many European based instructors who clinicked in America were known for their gruff Gestapo-like tactics that made fear run through the veins of their students. Would our new Swedish mentor impatiently slap the whip against his boot with critical demands that were impossible to satisfy?

Our misgivings were quickly dispelled the opening session when we were welcomed into the arena by a ruddy smile and a hearty Swedish "Halla". Despite broken English that required everyone to listen a little harder, it was evident from our first meeting that the Major was a master communicator. While some

Down the Aisle

of the riders struggled to understand his phraseology, there was definitely no language barrier with the horses who instantly embraced his meaning whenever he borrowed their reins to personally clarify a point. As he emphasized in each lesson, "Every horse has something new to teach you. Be sure to listen."

The needs of the horse were always put first with great emphasis placed on fairness. From this foundation, he took us back to traditional basics, underscoring the value of patient training progression. This was clearly evident in one of his favorite sayings, "T-T-T. Things take time. T-T-T. Listen to the letters chime and do not forget."

Major Lindgren was the consummate professional whose inspiring lessons became the basis of my teaching philosophy.

Down the Aisle

For that special Symposium week in July, we immersed ourselves in the rarified atmosphere of the Major's systematic training that utilized creative gymnastic exercises and clever imagery to permanently embed his message into our consciousness. His signature technique was the use of bright orange traffic cones to demarcate the patterns to be ridden. The baffling geometric maze that greeted us in the arena the first lesson evolved into an innovative, connect the dots system that improved precision and enhanced our navigational skills. The first purchase I made upon returning home to Sheboygan was a set of a dozen orange cones from the local sporting goods store. 38 years later those now faded, well-worn cones are still a valuable resource in my teaching arsenal.

Our memorable mentor definitely had a flair for description as evident in the many colorful expressions that overflowed the margins of my notebook. His to-the-point humor was expressed in phrases like "Buns management," "Play your instrument and conduct Bernstein with your supple wrists," "Shuttle the bits", "Sit straight and shine your breasts like headlights down the rail", "Let the joints of your fingers be oil cans to lubricate the horse's mouth" and "Hurry slowly". He had perfected verbal visualization to an art.

To this day, when one of my students is heavy in their hands, I still find myself singing aloud "Hanging in the Reins" which was the Major's adapted version of Gene Kelly's "Singing

Down the Aisle

in the Rain." It always has the amazing effect of causing the riders to instantly put their hands forward as I did so many years ago in response to his rich baritone notes. Ah, the persuasive power of song!

He was truly a teacher's teacher, the consummate professional who inspired each of us to leave the Symposium better instructors, infinitely more mindful of ourselves, our horses and our sport. By the end of that week every participant was a confirmed believer. The Major was definitely the real deal. Taking a line from the movie, Jerry McGuire, *he had us at "Halla."*

All of us new disciples fanned out across the country, eager to spread the gospel of the Major. We returned to our home farms, heads overflowing with what seemed to be the secret to life. Maybe it was just dressage, but to us it was equally as overpowering.

His message was a smash hit, making him quickly in demand for clinic tours across the country. The original faithful were joined by a growing legion of aspirants who flocked to the clinics, hungry to experience his message first hand. For the Major's part, his energy fed off the enthusiasm of this students as he built a trickle down pyramid system that educated the trainers who in turn educated their students in his philosophy.

He was taking the country by storm until a chronically painful hip caused by the wear and tear of a lifetime in the saddle inconveniently sidelined him. The doctors insisted he take a break from riding and his heavy travel schedule to have hip replacement

Down the Aisle

surgery. Outwardly, he bore the news with traditional military acceptance, while inwardly he was impatient to return to his beloved horses and waiting protégés. Unfortunately, complications from an unexpected infection necessitated a second surgery that left him permanently grounded. While travel and teaching would still be possible once he recovered, the doctor's prognosis for future riding was a resounding "NO" as it posed too great a risk to a hip joint that couldn't tolerate further injury.

With classic military grace, he accepted his new orders and soldiered on, not allowing his mission to spread his message to be dampened by this disappointing setback. Although his rebuilt hip restricted him from mounting the horses he loved, he was still determined to ride through his students. Despite physical limitations that prevented him from getting on to "fix" our horses, his vitality and encouragement still made us feel that he was sitting deeply in the saddle right behind our aids.

Over the next 14 years, I was fortunate to benefit from his coaching on a series of special horses. His wise words and encouragement helped me to discover the inner essence of each as no one else could. I remained a devoted follower, making twice annual pilgrimages to his clinic stops in Cleveland in the summer and Ocala, Florida in the winter. The sessions were incredibly motivating, populated by other ardent enthusiasts, all seeking reinforcement to the truths he had revealed to us. We talked, breathed and rode dressage from sunrise to sunset, unwilling to waste a single moment of the precious time. By the end of each clinic, we knew we had been elevated to a new level of comprehension and excellence.

The Major always swore he did not have a breed preference, insisting that a good horse was a good horse no matter what his stud book origins. However, I never failed to notice the way his eyes lit up at the mention of the breed of his homeland, so it was obvious that a little nationalism tugged at his heart. Intrigued by his undeclared breed of choice, I decided to research Swedish Warmbloods.

I discovered that the horses represented one of the oldest established breed registries in the world, based at the Swedish National Stud in Flyinge since 1661. Whereas many of the other warmblood breeds had evolved into riding horses from heavier agricultural types, Swedish Warmbloods had always been bred specifically for the mounted cavalry. The criteria necessary for a good military mount had resulted in the selective production of elegant, rideable horses with comfortable gaits and a positive, trainable temperament. At the time of my search in 1991, the Swedish Warmblood presence in the United States was so limited that the North American affiliated branch of the Flyinge-based breed was still in its formative stage.

From all accounts it sounded like my kind of breed, so when the time came in 1993 to search for a new youngster, I decided to look Swedish. A classified ad in *The Chronicle of the*

Down the Aisle

Horse describing an imported, four-year-old, bay Swedish Warmblood gelding caught my eye. A follow-up phone call located the prospect at a stable outside Annapolis, Maryland. I was informed that the horse was of the classic foundation bloodlines of Brisad – Utrillo. He was currently schooling first level with strong potential to move up the levels. Although he was an intriguing temptation, I hesitated as it was a very long way to travel for a horse that was at the very top end of my budget.

However, my vacillation elicited a familiar nudge in the back of my consciousness. It seemed as though my Guardian Spirit had reemerged, urging me not to walk from this one. At first I tried to ignore the nudge, but I just couldn't get the horse out of my mind. So, nothing ventured, nothing gained, by the end of the week I was booked on a flight to Baltimore with a rental car reserved to make the drive down to Annapolis.

All my uncertainties were laid to rest the moment the groom led the gelding out of the barn into the stable yard. I caught my breath at his commanding presence as the sun light reflected off the dapples of his rich mahogany coat. His classic topline was accentuated by an elegant neck, topped by a sculptured head bearing a regal, steady eye that told the world without a doubt that he knew who he was. He looked as though he had just stepped from the canvas of a fine oil painting. Certain that he was the most beautiful creature that I had ever seen, I wanted to pinch myself that such a horse could be in my barn.

Down the Aisle

"Steady," I reminded myself, focusing on the horse buyer's first rule of never letting the seller see you drool or babble in unintelligible excitement.

Trying to appear casually aloof while inside the butterflies were racing laps, I circled the gelding to inspect his legs. Of course they were unblemished as it never would do to have such a magnificent body marred by splints, puffs or scars. In answer to my questions regarding vices or health issues, his groom assured me he was equally perfect in body as well as soul.

There was nothing left to do but tack him up and follow the working student to the arena to watch her put him through his paces. The basic training on this youngster was all classically correct from his obedient acceptance of the rider's aids to his wonderful, metronome tempo at all three gaits. He was even more thrilling to experience once I was mounted.

Exhibiting the same inner confidence I had witnessed from the ground, he was light and responsive to my aids and always eagerly forward from the leg even though I was a strange rider. As we circled the arena with poised engagement, I was struck by what an incredibly long way I had come from the test rocket trial rides of my youth.

Beneath me flowed the promise of all I had trained so hard to become. I had learned well the lessons of my schoolmasters both human and equine. Now it was time to bring those tools to fruition on a talented young prospect of my own making.

Down the Aisle

Based upon the trial ride, I was certain that this horse could do it all. Of course, the widening grin that had consumed my face during the ride eliminated all hope of any bargaining power when it came to making a deal. But, as I was drunk on the thought of owning this magnificent creature, the money that I might have saved through clever negotiation seemed unimportant.

The only negative aspect of my beautiful new prospect was his registered name. Some foolish person had certainly misread the character of this splendid horse, labeling him with the totally inappropriate name of "Batman", conjuring up dark images of a masked, pointy-eared crime fighter. A name change was definitely high on the priority list. It had to be something extra special as I felt this Swedish horse exemplified the same attributes of honesty, strength of character and wisdom that I so admired in the Major. I was certain that if I applied his classical training system that this horse would reward me tenfold.

And, suddenly I was struck with the inspiration for the new name. It was so obvious that I immediately knew it was the perfect choice. I would name this wonderful Swedish horse "Anders" in honor of my revered Swedish mentor. Drawing upon his wisdom and lessons, I resolved to develop this talented young horse to hopefully one day again carry the name "Anders" down the centerline of the Grand Prix ring in tribute to the instructor who had given me so much.

Down the Aisle

I called to ask the Major's permission before submitting the necessary studbook paperwork that would make the name change official. There was a hesitation at his end of the line as he considered my request.

"Very good blood from Brisad and Utrillo. Both are strong lines with excellent dressage potential. And, is he handsome?"

"I've never seen such a beautiful horse," I quickly assured him. "The only thing more beautiful is his character."

On that promise, it was a done deal.

The gifting of "Ander's" name became official that January when I trailered my horses down to Ocala, Florida for my annual two week winter training session with the Major. To say I was nervous to witness his reaction to my new acquisition that bore his name was a huge understatement. Although the gelding had more than exceeded my glowing expectations during our first six months, the training time had been spent in the quiet environs behind my gate. I honestly wasn't certain how he would react to the unfamiliar excitement of the Florida facility.

All my concerns were put to rest by the conclusion of our first lesson. As though testing the integrity of his namesake, the Major put us through a challenging regime of exercises that far exceeded any questions I had previously put to my new horse. To the credit of my "Anders", he never faltered or balked, he just tried harder.

Down the Aisle

The Major studied us seriously at the conclusion of the lesson. The other riders and auditors clustered around the ring leaned closer, everyone anxiously waiting for him to pass judgment on his namesake.

"He is too damn obedient!" the Major finally declared. "Does he never make a mistake?"

He allowed the startled expression to freeze on my face for a moment before he winked and roared with satisfied laughter. "I think you have made a good choice, Leslie."

We concluded our Florida training session with a show in Clarcona to test the skills we had honed in our lessons with the Major. My new horse was to make his centerline debut at First Level. This would be another big "what if" hurdle as I had no idea how he would handle show pressures. Would he come unwound from the unaccustomed commotion? Would he become resistant from the stress and blow off my aids? All my uncertainties were put to rest as "Anders" willingly accepted the new challenges with his usual Zen like sensibility. Who ever would have thought that this green youngster would be the one taking the edge off my nerves at our first competition?

Down the Aisle

***Anders offered the promise
of all I had trained so hard to become.***

The Major came to the show grounds to coach the students who had been training with him. It was the only show of the year where I was fortunate to have his fine tuning input. "Anders" and I thrived on his advice, growing bolder and more confident with each movement. Much to my delight, the Major's coaching combined with my determination to please him resulted in a dream show.

Down the Aisle

I noticed the pride in the Major's eyes as he looked up toward the loudspeaker when "Anders'" name was announced for yet another win. He smiled fondly back at me. "Thank you for honoring me so with the name of this beautiful horse."

His thanks were unnecessary as it was the Major who had honored me for so many years with the generous gift of his wisdom and friendship.

Down the Aisle

Chapter Fifteen
Magnificent Garage Sale

One of the most complicated emotional relationships that defies definition is the triangle that develops between a girl, her horse and the man in her life, particularly when she grows into womanhood. From the earliest flicker of love pressed between a child's forehead and a pony's fuzzy forelock to teenage angst soothed by the nicker from a whiskered muzzle to a middle-aged woman inhaling the youth restoring elixir of horsehair, Vetrolin and saddle soap, they willingly and joyfully release themselves to the passion of horse fever.

To win a daughter's favor, a father delights in feeding her passion through equine indulgence ranging from riding lessons to the actual dream fulfilling purchase of a horse. However, when the time comes to hand off grown daughters and the resultant expenses of horse fever to prospective husbands, the poor new guy on the block is usually clueless to the magnitude of the equine condition. The uninitiated spouse-to-be can only scratch his head at the mysterious control the addiction has over his beloved not to mention the couple's purse strings.

Down the Aisle

As science has proven, the passionate neurotransmitters of new love start to fade by the end of a relationship's first year. Until the boil of passion begins to simmer into a less hormonal pattern, the freshly engaged male is quite game to be head cheerleader for any of his woman's pursuits, even taking an avid interest in horse activities that he never would have previously considered in his single, non-riding life.

However, the day ultimately arrives when the man perceives that his equine counterpart may be garnering an unbalanced amount of attention in their triangular relationship. Confronted by the lingering strokes and affection lavished on his four-legged competition, boyfriends, lovers and husbands can't be blamed for falling victim to the specter of jealousy that may raise its green head in a face off against the horse. From the significant other's perspective, the scales of emotional justice are certainly not equal when a horse is the counterweight.

Compared to the horse, men often feel they have received the very short end of the stick when it comes to receiving female sympathy and attention. For example, if the horse colics, the woman can be found tearfully walking her treasured companion for hours on end throughout the night, cooing unintelligible gibberish to soothe his stress. In the meantime, the vet bills are escalating well into the hundreds of dollars for farm calls, stomach tubing and IV fluids to hydrate the poor creature's depleted system. On the other hand, should the man complain of a belly ache from

Down the Aisle

a spicy, onion-laced German restaurant meal, he is unsympathetically handed a bottle of Pepto Bismol with the exasperated reprimand, "What were you thinking? You know better than to eat that." Certainly not a comparative scenario to endear the family horse to him.

Then, there is the case of the lost horse shoe thrown during a dewy pasture romp. Nothing for everyone on the farm to do but to put an immediate hold on all plans in order to slog through mud and ankle deep grass in search of the illusive piece of steel which is more than likely to resurface in the tread of the tractor tire the next time the husband mows the field.

And, finally, the most dreaded date on the horse husband's calendar is the obligatory holiday barn party. This annual ritual is an excuse for horse wives to exchange spur-strapped Dehners and leather-seated Pikeurs for the soft drape of cashmere and velvet. A night to let ponytails down into soft, highlighted waves that elicit delighted exclamations around the room of "Oh, you clean up so well!" But despite the festivities, once the introductions of "So, *this* is your husband" are complete and the pot luck buffet digested, the horse husbands can usually be found in a protective gaggle around the bar, sympathetically served by a like-minded host whose wife is holding court with her compatriots in the next room dissecting the latest stable gossip.

Confronted by all the evidence, horse husbands of the world may have a legitimate gripe in the definitive face off of

Down the Aisle

man vs. horse. Perhaps on that final Judgment Day of Reckoning, there might even be grounds for a sympathetic ruling in favor of the spouse.

Throughout the course of my 24 year marriage, Jeff like many horse husbands never truly grasped that equine love and human love were two entirely different emotions, capable from the woman's perspective of existing side by side without conflict in her heart. Although he smiled his support and publicly praised my equine efforts to family and friends, hidden beneath the surface my guitar playing, golf impassioned, retailer husband never really accepted my horses. Although refusing to openly admit it, to him, they were the competition whom he regarded as over-sized hay burners that vied for his wife's time and attention not to mention the frequent drain on our personal finances.

After our first eight years of marriage, Jeff reverted to humor to vent his unexpressed frustration with all things equine in a funky, folky song he composed entitled "The Magnificent Garage Sale." Written and performed tongue-in-cheek, it was guaranteed to get wild laughs from any audience as well as sympathetic nods from the male listeners who empathized with having an equally equine-attached spouse. The song fast became a special highlight of the annual holiday party always requested by the other horse husbands in the crowd.

The lyrics began "She bought chestnuts, she bought bays, she bought pintos, she bought grays, and 30,000 bales of golden

Down the Aisle

hay." The story song wound through the verses relating the poor husband's plight as his wife obsessively collected unimaginable numbers of horses. The chorus hook line quickly became a sing along with the men in the room enthusiastically booming out with Jeff, "Got no time for me 'cause I am not a horse."

Until one day, as the song continued, the downtrodden husband grabbed the opportunity to change his circumstances when his wife suffered a serious fall, "Yesterday her open jumper crashed her to the ground, stepped onto her collar bone, cracked with an awful sound. I became empowered, knew just what I had to do, advertising my Magnificent Garage Sale. I've got chestnuts, I've got bays, I've got pintos, I've got grays. And, if you'll only buy my horses, I'll throw in free 30,000 golden bales of the first stage of horse ..."

Freud would have had a field day with that material. However, every time Jeff performed it, I worked up a crooked smile to join in with the laughter and applaud his creativity along with the rest of the audience. I always sensed they were glancing sideways at me with a mixture of sympathy and amusement. But, I became proficient at returning a knowing nod, not wanting to acknowledge the true intent of the lyrics that threatened to derail the texture of my life.

For the next 16 years, our relationship drifted towards middle age as we individually pursued our vocations. At the end of most days, we still returned together over dinner to share the

Down the Aisle

fruits of our success as well as the disappointments of our defeats as we had since the early days of our marriage. Despite the gradual shifting of interests, I still found our relationship comfortable and comforting.

I guess I always assumed we would continue the partnership that we had pledged to uphold on that October day in 1972. "For richer, for poorer, in sickness and in health ..." But, reflecting upon those vows, I realized that Father Parker, our minister at St. Gregory's Episcopal, never did make any mention of horses in the service.

In 1996, the bottom dropped out of my world when Jeff unexpectedly announced, "This farm is dragging me down and sucking the life out of me."

My mind reeled. As far as I could fathom, there had been no recent outstanding incidents that warranted this unforeseen outburst. Maybe I should have had an inkling as there had certainly been subtle clues of discontent over the years, but I was truly shocked by his outright declaration. We weren't arguing, we never had. Maybe a little normal marital bickering over budgets and chores, but what long term relationship didn't have a few bumps in the road? I realized that in the past six months he had been working much longer hours at the store and there had been an increase in overnight company meetings, but that was about Sears not me.

Down the Aisle

"Where did that come from?" I protested, totally unprepared for the full blown power of his mid-life crisis. "You've never complained about being unhappy before."

Jeff gave a sad, facts-of-life shrug. "It's never been my way to make waves. I've tried to go with your flow for a long time, but I just can't live this way anymore. This whole horse farm thing has always been your dream, not mine. I want to have a little fun doing what I want with the rest of my life. And, it's just not this."

His mind and direction were firmly entrenched, leaving no room for discussion or negotiation. Unbeknownst to me, prior to his declaration of freedom from the farm, he had even arranged a pending job transfer to Raleigh, North Carolina that didn't include me in the house hunting. But, as the next few weeks would reveal, the horses were just an excuse for the affair he was having with an employee. He eventually declared that the woman who was 20 years his junior was also his 'true soul mate'. Guess that's where the "fun" he was looking for came in.

Jeff was quick to move out and on to the new life he was eager to forge in North Carolina. On the other hand, I felt paralyzed, reeling as my secure world that had been anchored by him since adolescence trembled in its foundations. Although I had always considered myself independent in thought and action, I now realized how much I had relied upon his support and advice throughout the years.

Down the Aisle

Now at 46 years of age, I found myself totally on my own. For the first time in my adult life, I had the sole physical and financial responsibility for a 10-acre farm that housed 10 demanding equine residents, three of whom were mine. While my teaching/training business was doing well, we had always relied on some resources from our joint incomes to cover major expenses such as the mortgage, taxes and insurance not to mention capital expenditures such as machinery and repairs. With Jeff's unexpected departure, the bottom was suddenly blown out of the farm budget.

I felt overwhelmed by my new responsibilities. Would I be capable of shouldering the whole weight of the farm? Could I stand alone? What were my prospects of staying afloat financially and emotionally yet still pushing my dream forward?

For several months, I tumbled toward what I didn't know, unable to control the speed or the direction. Friends and family tried to pull me out of my morass by pushing me along the antidepressant road to recovery, but the drugs only provided a temporary patch, not a cure to the overwhelming doubts that kept me down.

It was the aisle that finally broke my fall before I hit bottom. That wonderful corridor that had directed my life since childhood became a safety net that enveloped me within its walls, flanked by the wide, trusting eyes of my equine companions. Whenever I entered the aisle, they were waiting, long necks craned

Down the Aisle

out over dutch doors, inviting me into their embrace, letting me know I was needed.

My three current horses uplifted me through every step of my personal rebuilding with Anders the most intuitive of my boys. Every time I entered his stall, he would draw me and my tears into his big chest. If ever there was a period in my life when I needed a horse hug, it was then.

Dear, faithful Tusquin at 18 years of age had evolved from my personal mentor to lesson horse par excellence. The last few years of our competitive career he had developed respiratory complications that inhibited his breathing and stamina to work in a highly collected frame. Only one Grand Prix score short of earning my USDF Gold Medal, awarded for excellence at the highest level of the sport, my vet had suggested we try to improve Tusquin's breathing with tieback surgery in the hope of returning him to his winning ways in the show ring.

Unfortunately, the procedure was only partially successful, preventing a full return to Grand Prix form. With great disappointment I had to accept the reality that my much desired Gold Medal would have to wait until, if and when, I was ever lucky enough to be blessed with another equine partner who possessed the aptitude and talent for Grand Prix.

In the meantime, since Tusquin was still comfortable working at the lower levels, I started him on a whole new career educating my students to the finer points of dressage. As a steady,

Down the Aisle

dependable teacher, I welcomed him as my partner in this productive roll. I was certain he loved his new job almost as much as my students loved him.

While I was taking my time bringing Anders carefully up the training ladder, my current top competition horse was almost ready to fill Tusquin's shoes. Borne was a feisty, 11-year-old Dutch Warmblood gelding purchased four years earlier on a horse buying trip to Holland. He was a quirky, maniacal mad professor, but absolutely brilliant when he decided to put his mind to it. We were just ready to debut at Grand Prix when my personal world collapsed.

My healing time in the aisle made me realize that I could never forsake all that I had invested in the farm. I also couldn't let down my students who had loyally supported me through the turbulent days of the divorce. But, most importantly, I realized that I couldn't let myself down. I had worked too hard and sacrificed too much to walk away at this point in my life from all I had created just because of Jeff's mid-life crisis. As an old jump trainer who had coached me through what seemed an insurmountable course had declared, it was time to kick on for all I was worth to get over that next big fence.

It was my students who finally succeeded in coaxing me off the farm and back into the show ring. For a long time I was reluctant to leave the security of the safe bubble I had wrapped around myself behind the stable gate. However, I finally relented

Down the Aisle

to their persistent coaxing, allowing myself to be immersed in the luxury of their horse show enthusiasm. They were right. I needed to push away from the sadness and get back out there if I was going to heal completely.

In April, our trailer convoy composed of six horses, riders and assorted supporters headed north to a favorite show held at Lake Erie College in Painesville, Ohio. I had to admit that I welcomed the familiar comfort of the well-known show routine of schooling and correcting, braiding and brushing to fine show ring sheen. The total concentration of coaching each ride from beginning to end was definitely a healing elixir.

And, then, it was finally my turn to compete. Borne was tacked and groomed to a glistening burnished copper. In the warm-up, he was eager and quick to my aids as we prepared to enter the ring for his debut Grand Prix.

Amazingly, as we turned down the centerline, cantering forward toward the entry halt at X, all the paralytic doubts and worries of the past months melted away beneath his bold strides. Throughout the test, my fiery chestnut powered me to a fresh level of confidence and excellence beyond any I had previously experienced.

As we flowed effortlessly through the movements, I was acutely aware that my partnership with this wonderful, brilliant horse had finally set me free. No matter how deep I had tumbled into the abyss of divorce, I finally realized that I could soar far

Down the Aisle

above any emotional obstacle if I just allowed my horses to carry me on their broad wings. Where spousal rejection had overwhelmed me with self doubt, Borne's unconditional love and totally committed performance empowered me to believe in myself again.

My partnership with Borne set me free to believe in myself again after the divorce.

Down the Aisle

If the thrill of Borne's test had not been curative verification enough, the announcement over the loudspeaker iced it. Not only had we won the Grand Prix, but his score had been high enough to earn my long sought after Gold medal. The announced results for the placings of the rest of the class were drowned out beneath the joyful whoops of my students.

Down the Aisle

Chapter Sixteen
Shared Horizons

Shared passion is always more satisfying than solo experiences. The hopes, fears and aspirations of the aisle are most richly experienced with barn buddies or significant others who represent a much needed supportive audience and sage sounding board. There are few comforts better than a paneled tack room on a chilly December day where a circle of friends clean the grime from bridles and souls over thermos coffee and brownies. Or kindred spirits leaning against a four-board fence, sharing an understanding ear and the sight of horse buddies grazing muzzle to muzzle, nostrils deep in spring grass. Or a spouse's firm, all encompassing hug at the loss of a treasured companion.

Equine camaraderie takes many forms. Those of us inflicted with high doses of horse fever tend to imbue our four legged partners with an elevated anthropomorphic status. We look them square in those soft brown eyes, wrap our arms around their muscular necks then spill out our hearts, trusting their loyalty to maintain treasured secrets. Many a horsewoman's most important life decisions have been resolved by a pocket nuzzle or a late night nicker.

Down the Aisle

Beginning with the days of Jambalaya, I had considered horses my most reliable confidants. However, as I tried to adjust to my new status as single, middle-aged, horse farm owner, I quickly realized my soul still craved a deeper, personal connection that went beyond what my horses could provide. While during the day my aisle overflowed with the friendly chatter of clients, each night when the last car drove out of the gate and I put the stable to bed, loneliness settled in like a heavy fog.

After pulling the Kentucky doors shut, I found myself turning to open the door of an empty, dark house. Flicking on the lights, there was no longer a welcoming face with whom to share the day's trials and joys. No one to calm my rants about Borne blocking me in piaffe, or to celebrate my over the top elation of Ander's first clean flying change, or to sympathize with the irritation of the new student's inability to arrive on time for lessons. Even if the horses hadn't been Jeff's thing, throughout the years he had successfully masked his disdain while supporting me through good times and bad.

My aging Malamute, Aspen, represented my only late night companion. However, I was certain that she secretly blamed me for the divorce. Months after the departure of Jeff and his personal effects, she was still off her food, pining for his return. No amount of beef jerky temptations could cheer her. Stationed at the back door until all the lights were turned out, she would throw me "the

Down the Aisle

look" over her shoulder whenever I had the audacity to pass her mourning post.

Despite the evening loneliness, I didn't hold out much hope for change. It seemed a very remote possibility that there could be a man out there who was eager to embrace me and my very demanding horse farm lifestyle. And for my part, I was not interested in making a mid-life course correction. At 46 years of age, I was too deeply invested in my horses and profession to walk away from it for love.

However, some of life's greatest delights derive from being proven wrong as I was that summer of 1996. While my personal life remained in disarray, the professional aspects were reenergizing when eight of my students and I trailered north to compete in the N.O.D.A dressage show at Chagrin Valley Farms outside Cleveland.

I was standing beside the warm-up ring schooling a student when Doug approached. He was a casual horse show acquaintance who never failed to make me smile with a clever story or a joke. Our paths crossed companionably several times a year during the show season. He was an independent businessman who dabbled as an amateur dressage rider on the weekends, while his professional wife operated a high end Warmblood import business from their home training stable.

He gave me a curious look as he leaned back against the fence. "Guess you heard about my divorce."

Down the Aisle

I nodded, not taking my eyes off my student.

Even though I had kept myself fairly well sequestered behind my farm gate over the past few months, news tinged with the potential for gossip had spread rapidly through the horse industry long before modern internet connections. The current buzz was that Doug had just come out of a nasty divorce initiated by his English immigrant wife. After seven years of marriage, his spouse had decided to permanently keep her heart and horses in Florida at the end of the winter circuit where an aging dressage icon had caught and kept her eye. Whereas her marriage to Doug had provided her a green card and a base of operations for her burgeoning business, this new relationship promised greater horse glory.

I mustered a sympathetic smile. "Really sorry. From what I heard, you've had a tough time. Now that you're on the other side, maybe you can give me some advice because I'm in the middle of a divorce myself. To be honest, I'm finding life quite overwhelming when I try to do anything except the horses."

And, as they say, the rest was history. The next weekend Doug began a determined quest to change both our personal fortunes. He initiated his master plan with a three hour drive to Columbus, offering me friendly advice over an Italian dinner at Bravo's. That night, much to both our surprise, we closed down the restaurant with conversation fueled by laughter, pasta and

Down the Aisle

Chianti that hinted at a relationship far beyond platonic ringside friendship.

The deal was clinched when Doug took me home. I invited him in for a cup of coffee to keep him alert on his late night drive back to Cleveland. While he waited on the sofa for the pot to brew, Aspen surprisingly relinquished her back door mourning post to curl at his feet. Watching her tail softly wag I couldn't believe my eyes as she basked in his easy affection. When Doug asked me for a follow-up date the next weekend, I said "yes" for my sake as well as Aspen's. After months of suffering her broken heart, who was I to deny my dog's future happiness as well as what just might be mine?

Aspen may have had her personality quirks, but she certainly knew how to pick the right partner for us. As the months progressed, Doug proved his devotion by embracing me and the farm's needs. Most weekends he could be found happily draped in the Full Cry Farm banner. If we were at a show, he would cheerfully tag along, providing invaluable grunt work support as well as cheerleading me and my troops. If I was teaching at home, he would slip into handyman mode, tackling fix-er-upper projects from wiring to woodworking that had fallen by the wayside.

Before long, his steadfastness combined with a true love of all things equine had won a permanent place in my heart. I was delighted to realize that he too was possessed by a full blown, genuine case of horse fever. He didn't even try to disguise it behind

Down the Aisle

a facade of male bravado as he snuggled happily with my horses, doting on their accomplishments no matter how insignificant.

When we were ready to move our relationship on to the next level, it only seemed fitting to seal the commitment by entering into a new horse project that would make us partners in the tack as well as in the heart. My friend in Maryland, importer of Swedish Warmbloods extraordinaire, guaranteed she had just the right youngster to suit my needs. With that promise, Doug and I headed off to Annapolis on our first equine adventure.

Doug became my devoted partner at Full Cry Farm, sharing the pleasure of a Sunday morning ride on Anders while I rode Dauntless.

I knew the moment I saw the black, three year old gelding I knew he was something very special. He had recently been

Down the Aisle

imported from the Flyinge, the State stud of Sweden, where he had been a young stallion candidate. As he surveyed us from the end of the lead rope, he possessed all the ego and bravado of a recently gelded colt. Son of the world renowned dressage champion, Edinburg, his stunning physical presence conveyed all the promise of his famous sire. Doug and I mutually caught our breath as the groom trotted him off for our inspection. His floating, raw power gave me goose bumps.

If my business sense was captivated by his potential, the moment I touched him, my heart was captured by his engaging personality. For all his regal bearing, in the hand he was a goofy, affectionate clown who would have crawled into my jacket pocket in search of treats if he could have found a way to fit.

Everything about him suited my dream criteria except his name, Jablonski. My importer friend explained that the breeder had named him in honor of Henryk Jablonski, a Polish socialist and freedom fighter member of the French resistance during World War II who had gone on to become President of the People's Republic of Poland in the mid-70's – 80's. Certainly a notable, historic figure in Europe, but a show announcer's nightmare in the States where his identity and its pronunciation were almost certain to be unknown.

As I watched the groom release the gelding to bound playfully across the paddock, Doug squeezed my hand. I knew without asking that he genuinely shared my passion for this horse

Down the Aisle

and the roll he would play in our future. In that moment, I realized that the only appropriate name for this wonderful new horse was Horizon as he represented the bright promise of all that awaited Doug and me down the aisle.

Down the Aisle

Chapter Seventeen
Czarina of all Equine

The little timber-framed stone barn had stood sturdy and snug against the elements in Sjobo, Sweden for three generations of Sandburg family horse breeders. Five big box stalls always bedded deep with clean straw had welcomed a succession of Swedish Warmbloods that had all stemmed from Gustav Sandberg's original foundation mare, Marsipan.

Located in the heart of horse country near the Flyinge, the State stud of Sweden, the Sandburg family breeding program had enjoyed easy access to notable bloodlines. The list of top sires who had been selected for their mares included Napoleon, Flamingo, Drabant, Magini and, most recently Edinburg, the sire of newest filly born in the farm's foaling stall.

Eva Sandburg was particularly fond of the dainty, black filly as she realized this filly would be the last in a line of fine dressage foals produced by her beloved mare, Malva. This was the mare's first cross to Edinburg, a champion Russian Trakehner who had competed internationally under Kyra Kyrklund and then was approved for breeding by the Swedish Warmblood

Down the Aisle

Association to stand at the State stud. It had been an especially significant breeding choice as Edinburg had died unexpectedly the previous fall so this filly would be representative of his final foal crop.

Fulfilling Eva's hopes, Malva had produced a petite, sculpted mirror image of the famous sire. Even as a weanling, the filly exhibited a regal presence as if announcing to the world that she was the Czarina of all equine. Her natural aristocratic bearing had inspired Eva to name her Anastasia to reflect her Russian heritage as well as the mystery that had surrounded Czar Nicholas II's youngest daughter.

Eva's health had been failing for several years with a diminishing long term prognosis. A widow without children to assume the mantel of the little breeding farm, she knew it was time to stop thinking about selecting the next stallion match for Malva. A cousin near Lund had a stall waiting for Malva's retirement once this filly was weaned. Now there was just enough time left for Eva to focus on finding a special home for her final foal.

A recent phone call from a trainer friend had hinted at a promising solution. Pelle had been searching the 1999 Swedish Warmblood foal crop for a suitable Edinburg offspring for a client in the States who had contacted him specifically interested in this bloodline. The American was planning a trip to Sweden in November to look at foals from Edinburg's final foal crop. Pelle

Down the Aisle

thought Eva's filly might be a good prospect for his client if she was interested in selling.

Content in her pasture, Anastasia was unaware that her heritage was about to play a big role in determining her future. Life so far had been without demands or fears. She basked in the love and security of her nurturing dam's universe. Malva nuzzled her flank when she nursed or stood watch over her when she napped in the lush grass. The mare even good-naturedly tolerated the filly's nips and butts when the she overflowed with youthful exuberance.

Anastasia's days began and ended with a woman who spoke to her in a quiet, pleasant voice. She had wide, gentle hands that always seemed to satisfy the itches over the filly's hips. Each day the woman with the comfortable smell of soap and coffee would lead her and Malva to and from the field as well fill up their feed tub with tasty grains and hay.

Initially, Anastasia had been curious about this human who she noticed watching her for long, thoughtful periods over the pasture fence or stall door. But, with time, the woman blended into the background of the farm scenery just like the wheelbarrow that delivered breakfast hay or the tractor that removed manure from the stable or the shaggy brown dog who barked outside the fence whenever she and her dam romped in the field.

Idyllic days overflowed into a rhythmic routine for Anastasia on the quiet little farm at the end of the long, tree lined

Down the Aisle

gravel lane until one chilly, windswept morning in November, 1999. From the far side of the pasture, the shaggy dog barked to announce the arrival of visitors. Anastasia and Malva paused from grazing to watch a big, black car pull into the stable yard. Three unfamiliar humans bundled in bulky coats and wooly hats climbed out. The woman with the gentle hands greeted them and led them to the pasture fence, pointing in Anastasia's direction.

At the sight of her mistress, Malva pricked her ears and trotted eagerly toward the gate as visitors usually had pockets full of treats when they came to admire one of her babies. Anastasia stuck cautiously close to her flank, knowing Malva would protect her if there was danger. While she too was curious, she was not as confident as her dam to trust the outstretched hands that tempted with bits of carrot.

The visitors slowly entered the field, babbling a strange language unfamiliar to Anastasia's ears. While she did not understand their words, the language spoken by the woman with the gentle hands had begun to gain some meaning. There was "morotin" for the delicious sweet, orange vegetables that were now being offered, or "sot flicka" whenever the woman gently stroked her, or "Bra!" when she clapped her hands in exclamation of good behavior. But, the words uttered by the strangers had odd sounds spoken too quickly to make sense.

Anastasia kept a safe distance, tentatively craning her neck around Malva's wide chest. She tilted her head to check out the

Down the Aisle

interlopers in her pasture, filling her nostrils with their unfamiliar scent. Warily scanning each human, her eyes finally came to rest on one face that particularly held her interest.

Caught in her spell, I returned Anastasia's gaze with the same curious amazement. I dared not move in case the spell be broken and the filly dart off across the field. After eight long months of waiting, I was finally making the acquaintance of the current object of my equine desire.

From a windswept Swedish field, Anastasia and I embarked on a remarkable journey.

Down the Aisle

Our meeting in that blustery Swedish field had not even been a footnote in my business game plan a year prior. At that time, I was pleased with the promise and trainability of my Edinburg gelding, Horizon. Based upon our relationship, I had hoped to bring along another young Edinburg offspring sometime in the distant future. But, as the saying goes, "The only thing constant is change."

Edinburg's untimely death in 1998 had unexpectedly thrust my timetable ahead at warp speed. While my horse budget at the time was definitely not in a state to afford one of his mature offspring, I decided to search for a foal from his upcoming and final foal crop as a more viable option. The only hitch was that the majority would be born in Sweden.

In February, 1999, I elicited the aid of my friend and Swedish Warmblood importer par excellence in the task of searching for a suitable prospect. One of her Swedish agents was a friend of Eva Sandburg. He suggested the promising bloodlines of the foal carried by her mare, Malva, who had been bred to Edinburg. Based upon his recommendation and the urging of my friend, in April I began a Malva foal watch from Ohio. It continued to occupy my imagination right up until the agent's phone call on June 30 announcing the birth of the little black filly.

A filly?!? In all the weeks of waiting and wondering about the prospects of Malva's soon to be delivered foal, it never crossed my mind that she would produce a filly. That just did not fit the

Down the Aisle

scenario I had planned for my next horse. I was definitely a gelding girl. No hormonal mare hissy fits for me.

Spellbinder had been my one and only mare. While I treasured her memory, I knew I had been lucky to dodge the hormone bullet with her. Through all our experiences, she had proven to me that a truly great mare was great horse often better than the boys she competed against. I also knew from years of experience with client horses that those extra special girls are few and far between. I wasn't eager to tempt fate a second time.

Yet here I stood, eye to eye with one of the most stunning little creatures I had ever beheld. She was a petite female version of her sire, right down to the beautiful long neck and sculpted head. The months of anticipation, the long flight to Sweden, and the concern over her sex all evaporated in that moment as she held my gaze, head cocked slightly to take me in with huge, full eyes.

If it hadn't been for the circumstance of Edinburg's untimely demise, I would never have considered purchasing a weanling. While many youngsters had graced my aisle over the years, at a minimum they had been three-years-old and ready to begin training toward a career. All my years of experience had not prepared me to deal with so young a filly. But, here in her presence, I was captivated by her aura. The desire in my heart easily overruled the logic that my head was trying unsuccessfully to communicate.

Down the Aisle

I had to admit that in a back corner of my imagination I had always harbored a secret desire to own a special mare for whom I could someday select the ideal stallion. My selective chemistry would be instrumental in the creation of the ultimate horseman's fantasy of taking a victory gallop lap on the back of my own sport horse creation. It had crossed my mind with Spellbinder, but the timing had been wrong, so the opportunity was lost. After her with only geldings in my aisle, the breeding dream had faded. But now, captivated by this magnificent filly flanked by her wonderful dam, my imagination began to bubble.

I carefully extended my palm toward the filly's tiny teacup muzzle. Instinctively, she drew back behind her dam. But, before spinning on her heels to flee, she hesitated. Never taking her eyes off me, she cautiously arched her neck to its full length, exhibiting amazingly regal bearing for such a youngster. Nostrils flared, she tentatively brushed my fingertips with her whiskers. The brief contact triggered a high-pitched squeal that sent her charging off across the pasture with Malva close on her heels.

Our little group watched in admiration as mare and foal circled the field. Anastasia boldly held the lead, leaping and fishtailing with joyous abandon. Exhibiting such freedom and natural suspension to her stride, I was certain the next moment she would surely take flight from the earth's bounds.

There was nothing more the agent or Eva needed to say to convince me of Anastasia's merit. The filly had clearly sold herself

Down the Aisle

to my heart. I couldn't imagine my aisle without her sparkling presence.

The purchase of the filly represented the closest I had come to beginning the training process from the ground floor. The prospect was at once exciting and quite overwhelming. Who knew where the future would lead us? At that moment, there were no limitations, only possibilities. The little Czarina and I were about to embark upon a remarkable journey the outcome of which neither of us could have imagined that day we first met in a windswept Swedish field.

Down the Aisle

Chapter Eighteen
Making Magic

Meredith fixated on the fat, terrycloth calico pony dangled tantalizingly over the side of the crib by great aunt Lena. Her chubby baby hands eagerly grasped its tail, pulling the soft toy into her chest. Without a moment of hesitation, she began sucking contentedly on its ear, triggering a lifetime of equine desire.

With the progression of childhood years, bedroom surfaces became cluttered with red, brown and black plush horses, yarn manes braided, combed and waved. Bedside bookshelves were stuffed with volumes ranging from Marguerite Henry stories to Walter Farley's **Adventures of the Black Stallion.** Even her mattress sat atop a mural of blond, pig-tailed cowgirls astride rearing, galloping and pawing palominos who circled the perimeter of the box spring. If horse fever was truly an addiction of little girls, Meredith was sorely afflicted.

As she grew, stuffed toys and story tales were soon not enough to satisfy a burning desire for ownership of a real live horse. In pursuit of her quest, she engaged in all the normal childhood parental manipulations ranging from begging to pouting

Down the Aisle

to volunteering slave labor around the house until her parents finally relented.

A favorite Dorothy Lyon's novel, **Red Embers**, long displayed in a prominent place in her bedroom library provided the inspiration for naming her new chestnut companion. Denmark's Red Embers quickly became shortened to "Emby" as the inseparable pair ranged the countryside in search of adventures.

The year Meredith turned 16, her parents decided it would be a good educational experience as well as an investment to breed the Saddlebred mare. When "Emby" came into spring heat, Meredith swung up on her bareback and jogged seven miles down the road to leave the mare with a neighbor's stallion. Without relying on science or technology, the mare was turned out with the stallion to be pasture bred. When Meredith returned five days later to ride "Emby" home, Mother Nature and blind luck resulted in a pregnancy on the first breeding.

340 days later, Meredith experienced the miracle of foaling as she assisted in the delivery of a golden chestnut filly with four white socks. Although "Emby" and her filly had to sadly be sold to help defray college tuition expenses, the momentous event of the foaling convinced Meredith that this must someday be her destiny.

Meredith first entered my aisle in 1998 when she stopped by to inquire about dressage lessons. Our initial meeting was one of those rare instant connections that promises to blossom far past the intent of the initial contact. As our friendship grew beyond the confines of the teaching arena, I learned she was the proprietor of a veterinary clinic dedicated to the treatment of cats. The successful practice had allowed her to fulfill her adolescent dream that had long been on hold since the sale of "Emby".

Finally in a financial position to turn dream into reality, Meredith had purchased 35 open acres to begin breeding Holsteiner horses under the banner of Meridian Farm. Her foundation mare was a chestnut Thoroughbred named Suzie Cutie who had endured 126 races over eight grueling years on the track before retiring to be sold as a broodmare prospect. Her conformation, proven stamina and wide searching eyes had won Meredith's heart as the ideal candidate to cross with Holsteiners to produce modern type show jumpers. In due time, Suzie Cutie had rewarded her new owner's faith by foaling a string of fine colts and fillies destined to make their mark in the show ring.

It was Meredith to whom I turned for advice and moral support when I made the decision to breed Anastasia. Although my mare had been broken and lightly ridden for six months, a pasture injury as a yearling had resulted in a slight, permanent hitch in her right hip. While Ana remained serviceably sound for pleasure riding, a competition career was definitely out of the question due to the gait irregularity.

As breeding had been a someday dream since her purchase, I now redirected aspirations for my mare toward that goal. When

Down the Aisle

Anastasia turned three, to fulfill her breed association's requirements, we attended the Swedish Warmblood's annual breed inspections in Cleveland. Braided and groomed to a high, black sheen, she showed herself off with the elegance of a true czarina, earning glowing praise from the judges. Much to my delight, they awarded her the top rating of Class 1, including a 9 for type. Encouraged by the enthusiastic evaluation of the judges, I began the search for the ideal stallion.

Once the decision had been made I found myself in the daunting position of a novice breeder breeding a novice mare. Anastasia and I were both definitely rookies in this area. While I had all the confidence in the world to start a young horse under saddle, train flying changes or meet the demands of a jumping gymnastic, I was a total neophyte when it came to horse breeding. Newborn foals were definitely adorable, never failing to trigger my "ah" response, but admiration was the limit of my breeding expertise. Five decades in the horse industry had left a definite gap where I was currently most in need of knowledge.

As the time approached to breed Anastasia, Full Cry Farm was uprooted yet again this time to accommodate Doug's job transfer. When he initially proposed the move to Cincinnati, I immediately balked. After all, I had a successful business in Columbus and a strong network of friends who had seen me through some very difficult times. One of the positive things that had come out of my divorce from Jeff was also a divorce from the constant relocation policy. No more Sears meant no more moves which equated to finally being able to establish permanent roots. I had celebrated my corporate separation by planting Bradford pear trees down my driveway, relishing the opportunity to see them grow to maturity.

Doug and I were still newlyweds, barely a year into our marriage. He had sold his home in Cleveland and moved to Columbus with his two Labradors to join me and Aspen on my farm.

Much as I loved my home, I had to admit that it still harbored so many memories of my life with Jeff from the artwork that adorned the walls to the antiques we had collected since college days. I suddenly realized that the house was so filled with memories past that there wasn't a lot of room for memories future with Doug.

Maybe it was time to consider a totally fresh start, to create a new farm that was purely Doug's and my vision. "All right," I finally agreed. "Much as I don't want to go through the hassle of another move, I'm willing to do it one more time because I think we owe it to our relationship to have a truly fresh beginning. However, this is indisputably my final move, so we better get it right."

And we definitely did, creating our dream farm out of 15 virgin acres of corn just east of Cincinnati in Stonelick Township. Starting from bare ground, we raised a 10-stall barn with attached

Down the Aisle

indoor arena and outdoor dressage ring. The design for the ranch house with views of big, grassy paddocks from every window had been tucked away for years in the back of my imagination just waiting for the right time to be built.

Like many of my long established Columbus clients, Meredith willingly made the two hour commute to the new, improved Full Cry Farm #7. I was happy to see her continue lessons as she now also wore the mantel of my personal reproduction guru, generously imparting valuable advice on stallion selection, genotype, artificial insemination and breeding soundness exams just to mention the highlights.

I gratefully deferred to her expertise. "You are so good at this, my sage friend. Thanks to you, the science of breeding is starting to make sense. You really should think about writing a book to simplify the process for all us rookies. Think of the frustration and worry, not to mention money you could save us."

"I've thought about it many times," Meredith admitted. "But, I'm just not an experienced enough writer to tackle a book."

In the pause that followed, inspiration struck. It had been nearly 30 years since the publication of my juvenile novel, *Tic-Tac*. Over the years, I had published a few short stories and poems, but my imagination hadn't caught fire on another promising book project. I genuinely missed writing, but through the years, marriage and horses not to mention the Midwest Horse Fair had swallowed up my free time. Without a motivating story line to shake the dust off my creativity, I ultimately fell out of the writing groove.

However, Meredith's admission presented me with an intriguing opportunity. I realized that this could be the story I had been waiting to write. Not only would I enhance my education into the stages of my mare's pregnancy, but I could interpret that knowledge from my layman's perspective to others in the same position.

"Meredith, if we work together, I think we can write that book you've always dreamed of," I offered. "You supply the scientific expertise and I promise to deliver the words. And best of all, Anastasia can be the heroine of our story."

That inspiration formed the foundation of our project. Twice a month for the duration of Anastasia's pregnancy, at the conclusion of Meredith's dressage lesson, we would adjourn to my kitchen table. There over lemon tea, Meredith would assume the teacher's role while I became the eager student, absorbing all she had to impart about equine reproduction.

Armed with a stack of textbooks interpreted by her years of experience as a veterinarian and sport horse breeder, she walked me through the stages of pregnancy from breeding to foaling that I in turn translated into layman's terms. At the end of each chapter, I detailed Anastasia's and my experiences under the heading "Personal Journey", opening a window to the reader of our specific circumstances.

Down the Aisle

"This whole process is really amazing," I remarked to Meredith early on in our partnership. "It's almost as though we're making magic."

From that simple declaration came the inspiration for the title of our book that was ultimately to be called *Making Magic: Breeding and Birthing a Healthy Foal.* Scientist that she was even Meredith had to agree that it was the perfect title.

The time following the inception of our partnership flew by. Before I knew it, the stallion we had selected as the ideal match for Anastasia successfully fulfilled his part of the contract on June 20, 2003 confirmed by a successful pregnancy ultrasound on July 9. Vivaldi was a 19-year-old internationally ranked Swedish Warmblood stallion. He had recently been imported from Sweden to stand at Three Crowns Farm in Woodinville, Washington. A top sire of F.E.I. dressage horses, he was noted for producing superior gaits and conformation. Although initially I had concerns about fertility at his age, the breeder assured me he still had a 79% conception rate from shipped, fresh-cooled semen. With that data in hand, Meredith had given the match two resounding thumbs up.

Now after 11 months of studying, writing and rewriting, not to mention nurturing my blossoming pregnant mare, all that remained to resolve the final chapter of the book was the birth of her much anticipated foal. According to the scientific average of a 340 day equine pregnancy, Anastasia's due date was May 26,

Down the Aisle

but anyone who owns a mare knows that predictability is often not in their nature, especially with a first foal.

However, my much pampered czarina must have realized that literary immortality depended in part on a good photo shoot to record the big event for the book. Not one to miss an opportunity for fame, Anastasia clearly let me know that she was going into first stage labor at 5 a.m. the morning of May 24, 2004.

Throughout the pregnancy, a barn cam had been directed on Ana's stall, allowing me to monitor her condition from the house without disrupting her peace. For the past month, her stall light had been left on throughout the night so I could check her on the bedroom television. Those overnight checks of my ever peaceful girl had increased in frequency until I think I spent well more time watching her peacefully sleep on the screen than counting sheep myself.

On May 24, my 5a.m. wake-up intuition witnessed a very different scene. Rather than sleeping against the stall bars nose to nose with Tusquin, Anastasia was circling uneasy laps, occasionally flagging her tail before settling back beside Tusquin. When her restless pattern became repetitious, I knew our wait was nearly over.

I shook Doug out of a deep sleep as I sprang into action on the heels of Mother Nature. "This is it! See you in the barn. Don't forget the camera. We need those birth shots for the book."

Down the Aisle

Once a visual check assured that my increasingly agitated mare was truly in labor, I called the vet. Much to my dismay even at this early hour, he was already out on an emergency with another one waiting.

"You'll be fine," he assured after listening to my detailed description of the situation. "Sounds like everything is progressing normally. Anastasia may be a maiden, but nature will tell her what to do. I'll do my best to get over there before noon. Gotta go. Good luck."

I stared at the phone in disbelief that was rapidly morphing into dread. I had never witnessed a foaling except on video tape let alone served as the primary foaling attendant. Even though I had spent the past year writing about the procedure, pen and paper were no substitute for hands-on experience.

I had always taken it for granted that when the big moment arrived I would assume the role of proud owner watching from the sidelines while an experienced vet and my mare worked together to deliver a healthy foal. Never had I imagined that neophyte me would have to serve as Anastasia's midwife, holding as a guide book the manuscript that I had written. Not a comforting thought!

It was definitely time to call in the cavalry. "Meredith!" I exclaimed when she answered the phone. "Help! Ana's in first stage labor and my vet is four hours out on an emergency. I'm not sure I can do this alone."

Down the Aisle

Meredith instantly became a font of calming encouragement. "Of course you can. Besides, you won't be alone. I'll keep my cell with me in the clinic so you can reach me anytime with questions. Have faith that Ana will manage just fine. Mares have been doing this on their own for a long time. Now, describe to me what she's doing."

I glanced out the open stall dutch door where Doug was hand grazing Anastasia to ease her growing restlessness. "She's quiet right now. Once she got out of the stall to nibble a little grass, she settled down."

"That's good," Meredith agreed. "Just keep an eye on her. When she breaks a sweat, it's just about time for the foal to arrive."

I looked at my dear, swollen bellied mare who could barely waddle between patches of grass. A year ago this project had seemed like a terrific idea, but now I seriously wondered what could have possessed me to put both of us through this uncertain ordeal.

"Calm mare, no sweat," I reported to Meredith, but almost as quickly I noticed a new glisten on Ana's neck when she turned to catch the rising sun's early rays. "Oh, my gosh, there is sweat! I know it wasn't there a minute ago. What should I do now?"

"Get that girl back inside right away unless you want to have that foal in the field," Meredith firmly directed. "Once she's settled in the stall call me back."

Down the Aisle

My dear friend and birthing mentor was good to her word. Never more than one phone ring away, throughout the morning she guided my actions and hands in the delivery of a perfect, healthy filly who was a petite image of her dam except for a small white star.

Anastasia's newborn foal was pure magic for both of us.

Down the Aisle

"You did it!" my proud professor exclaimed as I described the newborn rolled up on her chest in the straw behind Anastasia. "I never had a doubt."

My vet and his assistant rolled in just before Noon to give the newborn and her adoring dam a thorough physical. Since Anastasia had streamed a great quantity of milk in the hours prior to the delivery, the vet was concerned that her foal had not received sufficient colostrum. As a precaution, he decided to administer 200ml of Seramune Equine IgG to the foal via nasogastric tube.

It took all available hands to accomplish this very invasive procedure on a tiny, strong willed foal who was determined not to participate. Everyone grabbed a piece of mare, foal or equipment and held tight despite a crescendo of thrashing and stomping protests. Sweat-stained and straw covered, we ultimately succeeded in delivering the Seramune in what I'm sure the filly considered a very rude welcome to her new world.

Late that evening when the emotions of the 19-hour-day had subsided and the barn had long gone to sleep, Doug and I sat outside the foaling stall basking in the sight of Anastasia nurturing her newborn. The delicate little filly slept full out beneath her adoring dam. I watched in amazement as my tough, independent mare turned into the poster child for maternal love. She delicately explored every inch of her foal, gently lipping each tiny hoof then carefully placing it back down in the straw with a noticeable sigh.

Down the Aisle

It certainly had been an overwhelming day, but in hindsight I wouldn't have traded a moment. All that remained was to name the new arrival. It had to be something special to convey the magnitude of the experience. The foal's mere presence and the implementation of all the steps that had brought her down my aisle were magic just like the title of the book we had written to journal her creation. And, in that moment, I knew that was the perfect name for my foal as well … Magic.

Down the Aisle

Chapter Nineteen
Vintage Defined

For nearly a decade, I had been categorized by the United States Dressage Federation as "Vintage". The descriptive title had been created by the organization for yearend awards classification. It was reserved for competitors who still managed to canter down the center line upon ripening to the mid-century mark of 50. Upon being crowned with the title, I wondered if it has been created to set mature senior riders apart from the pack with reverence, amazement or sympathy.

I couldn't help but shudder the day I finally crossed the "big" birthday threshold to earn my "vintage" designation and AARP card all in the same benchmark year. For the first time, I felt confronted by my own mortality. This grim thought was daily reinforced by print and broadcast propaganda, proclaiming I now belonged to a generation beset by a myriad of debilitating conditions including memory loss, weakened vision, incontinence, arthritis, high cholesterol, diminished libido and constipation.

It gave one pause to wonder how now that I was branded with the classification of "vintage" it was still possible to throw a

Down the Aisle

leg over the saddle, let alone pilot a 1,200 pound Warmblood around the ring. And still, I had to acknowledge, each season more and more of my peers who had seemed permanent fixtures around the show circuit had begun to replace well-worn saddles in favor of corner coaching stools. They seemed reconciled to bow to growing physical limitations, transferring their now ground bound dreams onto the shoulders of the youthful up-and-comers that they instructed.

I decided to enlist the help of my trusty, dog-eared Oxford dictionary for a precise definition of "vintage" to see how I had been pigeon-holed by the dressage community. The first listed definition, pertained to the production of grapes and wine. While I enjoyed a good cabernet, I don't think that's what the dressage powers had in mind with their selection of rider designation.

The second definition held more promise, "of high quality, especially from the past". Not bad. This definition was followed by "aged, seasoned, mature, classic". Instinctively, I drew a little taller. Maybe my newly crowned classification could actually be something to feel good about.

Then I arrived at a definition that really tweaked my newly achieved "senior" status in its ego. "Antiquated, old-fashioned, bygone, old-fogeyish." And, if that had not been enough to ram the "vintage" point home, at the end of the final definition listed as colloquial was "over the hill".

Down the Aisle

For the first time, I was forced to face the reality that in achieving the "vintage" title, I had also achieved the unthinkable and entered the Twilight Zone of what I had always considered my parents' generation. This was an almost unfathomable concept to a child of the '60's who had totally bought into the "forever young" culture. However, now as I studied my reflection in the mirror, I saw vestiges of my mother's face in the creases that had deepened in the outer corners of my eyes and mouth. For years, I had tried to shrug off the growing resemblance, but when a hint of my grandmother also began to creep into my visage, there was no denying that time was inevitably beginning to catch me in its grasp.

While teaching definitely occupied an enjoyable nitch in my life, I knew I wasn't ready to dismount and permanently retire to a corner coaching stool. However, I also recognized that physically there was not a lot of tread left on my tires. A lifetime of bumps and breaks had definitely taken its toll. The morning arthritic wake-up shuffle from the bed to the bathroom caused me to question with increasing frequency how much more my body could tolerate before the rigors of my sport evolved into rigor mortis.

And yet, deep in my core, I still tingled with the twinges of childhood glee from my Jumbalaya days at the anticipation of peering around the next open stall door to see what new opportunities it held. For years, parents and spouses had tried to

Down the Aisle

scratch away my obsession, but it had remained an insatiable itch. With so much more to feel and learn from the horses still waiting at the end of my aisle, it just wasn't time to dismount yet.

In the saddle for over five decades, I had never been one to buy into the latest "trick" or trainer du jour. The fad meisters may have bucked tradition with a quick fix to grab a temporary leg-up on the competition, but where were they 10, 20 or 30 years down the road? What was the long term value of short term gimmicks in a classical sport that had stood the test of centuries?

I had been blessed with genuine mentors who had instilled upon me the lessons of patience and perseverance. Whether equine or human from gentle to aggressive, nurturing to challenging, all had left a permanent thumbprint that defined the horsewoman I had become. And, in their long shadow, I felt the responsibility to question who in my turn would I define as I passed on the lessons of tradition to a new generation with an equally insatiable itch.

At what level would my passion touch theirs as I too became the thumbprint in another's memory? Would it be the backyard companionship of a sun-tanned cheek pressed into a shaggy chestnut mane? Who would hear my voice rhythmically counting the strides to a triple combination? Or feel my hand closing around theirs in demonstration of correct rein pressure for a half halt? It was a humbling responsibility of which I was appreciative whenever I walked into the arena.

Down the Aisle

I knew I had been blessed with the opportunity to spend a lifetime in the company of these magnificent creatures and the fraternity of people that were drawn to them. Before I acquiesced to being grounded to fulltime teaching, I still felt an important part of my future lay in rather than beside the saddle.

I had reached the fortunate age and stage in my life where I had the wisdom and luxury of being able to be selective in my choices. On the other hand, that venerable age also meant that I didn't have the benefit of youth's open ended time frame to return to the horse selection well countless times until I got it right.

The big question was what sort of horse would finally satisfy the itch that so many had tried to scratch? Over the years my passion had been blessed with a remarkable array of equine partners, each generously sharing their talents as well as their quirks. The four Swedish Warmblood companions who currently filled my stable comprised a wonderful mix of ability and personality. However, recent career redirections in my family of horses had left a gap in my saddle time.

Dear Anastasia, despite a slight hitch in her right hip, had matured into a solid, basic skills lesson horse, nurturing a string of devoted students while impatiently waiting for me to breed her again. Her five-year-old daughter, Magic, had just bonded with her dream human who was on track to becoming her new owner. Rasir, my top competition horse, had recently retired from Grand

Down the Aisle

Prix to assume an important new role as schoolmaster, moving from my riding to my teaching partner.

Despite a busy barn full of horses and boarders, I found myself down to only one serious daily ride. But upon reflection, of all the horses who had passed down my aisle, Dauntless came the closest to embodying the outstanding characteristics I had treasured over the years in my favorite mounts. If ever there had been an equine soul mate for me, it was my bright chestnut Swede. As brave as he was handsome, Dauntless had been my companion for six years, from the age of three until this season when he had put his hoof in the FEI ring for the first time.

The ideal solution going forward would be to clone him. But since my budget certainly wasn't that deep, the next closest genetic step would be to breed Anastasia to the sire of Dauntless. Don Schufro was a world-ranked stallion standing at the renowned Blue Hors Stud in Randbol, Denmark. Bearing the elite dressage bloodlines of Donnerhall and Pik Buba, the talented stallion had anchored Denmark's Olympic team to win the bronze medal at the 2008 Beijing Olympics.

On a recent horse shopping trip to Denmark with a client, we had the privilege to be invited to a private training session at Blu Hors to watch Don Schufro work with his partner, Andreas Helgstrand. Except for a slightly deeper liver tone to his chestnut coat, the similarity between Don Schufro's persona and my gelding's was uncanny. Captivated by the harmonious power that

Down the Aisle

propelled horse and rider across the arena, my goose bumps told me this was definitely the best opportunity to reproduce Dauntless through my mare.

*Dauntless was my equine soul mate
who never failed to make me smile.*

Down the Aisle

The biggest speed bump to the plan was the necessity to breed with frozen semen. As Don Schufro stood in Denmark, my only breeding option was unpredictable with a potentially much lower conception rate. Anastasia's first foal had easily been produced utilizing artificial insemination with fresh-cooled semen. However, the veterinary experts had advised me that she was not a good candidate for frozen semen due to complications that could arise from having a tight cervix.

Bucking science and logic, desire ultimately ruled the day as I decided to forge ahead with my idea. Realizing that the frozen semen route with Anastasia represented a breeding crap shot, I came to regard the project as the Las Vegas Plan. However, I resolved to push back if the plan proved unsuccessful by the time the allotted funds were depleted.

Giving the project every chance for success, I handed my prepped and willing mare over to the repro specialists at Rood & Riddle Equine Hospital in Lexington, Kentucky. There on May 5, 2007 at 9:00 pm under ideal conditions Anastasia was inseminated with Don Schufro's frozen semen that had been stored at the clinic for three months until just this perfect moment.

But, as with many best laid plans, mine was not destined to succeed as was confirmed by a negative ultrasound pregnancy check 16 days later. Although the vets suggested that statistically conception rates improved with each successive attempt, I remembered their initial reservations regarding my mare's poor

Down the Aisle

qualifications as a frozen semen recipient. Since the status of her tight cervix hadn't changed, I didn't see how further breeding attempts could improve my odds. It was time to cut the Las Vegas plan's losses and consider an alternative to finding a Dauntless "clone".

Did the qualities that I so loved in my gelding stem equally from his sire and dam, or did one parent contribute a disproportionate amount of phenotype? If Don Schufro wasn't a viable option, then what about Dauntless' dam, Nutella? Maybe the failed breeding attempt was my Guardian Spirit's way of telling me that I'd been looking at the wrong gene pool.

The registration papers for Dauntless noted that he had been foaled in April, 2000 at Bollerups Lantbruksinstitut in Tomelilla, Sweden. The agricultural institute was one of the premier breeding farms in Sweden, having produced many top horses including the international champion stallion Amiral who was a full sister to Dauntless' dam. But, seven years after Dauntless' birth, I wondered if Nutella continued to reside at Bollerups. Was she still alive? And, if so, had she recently produced any promising youngsters who fit my criteria?

Warming to the prospects of this new possibility, I set about contacting the young horse manager at Bollerups who assured me that Nutella was very much alive and still producing foals at age 14. In fact, he continued, she was the recent dam of a robust, bay stud colt by the stallion Richfield.

Down the Aisle

I wasn't familiar with the stallion, but I made a quick call to my go-to mentor Anders who was always an indisputable font of information regarding bloodlines. He told me that the promising seven-year-old Westfalen stallion had been approved and purchased by the Swedish State Stud. In 2006, Richfield had been named six-year-old Champion of Sweden. By 2008, the stallion was winning Prix St. Georges and Intermediare I classes on the international stage with bright prospects of Grand Prix looming in the near future. It certainly appeared that "Dad" had plenty of athleticism to supply to Nutella's new foal.

So far, so good, but I was quick to squash that familiar tingle of goose bumps as the new plan still had a lot of hurdles to clear before becoming reality. The next step was to request a video of the colt to see if the farm manager's promise lived up to my definition of exceptional potential.

If my interest had been tweaked by the initial contact with Bollerups, my hopes soared sky high when I viewed the video of the 2 ½ month old colt, trotting confidently at his dam's side. Bright-eyed, neck proudly up, he expressively threw out his shoulders as he floated across the screen. Watching the tape, I felt like a giddy child again, opening the best present ever. And I knew, before the video ended that he had to be mine.

Doug selected the perfect name to define the character of the newest member of Full Cry Farm. Needing a word beginning with an "R" to follow his sire's name, Doug suggested

Down the Aisle

Rickenbacker in honor of the famous World War I flying ace, Eddie Rickenbacker. I thought it was the perfect bold choice backed up by an interesting history.

Paperwork finalized, my bright new star had to remain at Bollerups until he was weaned at six months. From there he was sent to a private farm in Sweden for basic handling training to prepare him for shipment to the U.S. Once he could obediently be tied and led, it was time to make arrangements with the commercial shipper to finally transport him to Full Cry Farm.

His original ship date was mid-December in time for a Christmas arrival, but somewhere in the process his export documents slipped through the cracks of bureaucracy. The result was a long, frustrating delay as we waited for the required transport blood work to be completed for his passport.

Every Monday morning beginning in December, I would hopefully call the shipper's New York office only to hear, "So sorry, but still no blood work. Hopefully next week. We'll save a stall on the plane each week for him. As soon as we have the paperwork, he will be on his way to you."

There was nothing I could do from my side of the big pond but wait until the Swedish agricultural officials fulfilled the required protocol. Hard as I tried to relegate my dreams of the special little colt to the back of my consciousness for yet another week, it was like trying to tell a child that Santa had been delayed

Down the Aisle

until Easter. But, finally, 7 ½ months after his purchase date, the much awaited export passport was issued.

Rickenbacker arrived on U.S. soil the evening of March 11, 2008. The week of arduous travel had begun with my nine-month-old colt traveling ten hours from Sweden to the shipper's holding stable in Germany. Two days later, he was trailered to the Amsterdam airport to join a shipment of horses bound for the America. After three days in the USDA quarantine facility in New Bedford, New York he had finally begun the final 14 hour leg of his long journey to Full Cry Farm which had begun nearly a week earlier in Sweden.

Although I hadn't met the little fellow except on tape, my heart stressed for his wellbeing. Would he be overwhelmed by the strain of such a long trip? Would he be colicky and off his feed? Would his fragile immune system be jeopardized? Would he be nervous and shy from his experiences of passing through so many unfamiliar hands? I knew the toll this journey could take on an adult, experienced horse, but the risks were so much greater on a youngster. Poor little Rickenbacker was traveling solo.

On March 14 at 5:00 a.m., Doug and I waited in nervous anticipation as the big, commercial rig drove slowly down our farm drive. I think Doug was as excited as I over the arrival of our new addition. Over the months waiting for his importation, we had played out every scenario that could possibly pertain to the colt's growth and eventual prowess in the show ring. It had been

Down the Aisle

fun to let our imaginations run wild, but now reality was pulling into our stable yard.

I barely noticed the chill in the air as the trailer stopped in the glow of the barn vapor light. The driver climbed down, handing me the shipper's paperwork to sign while he fumbled with the van door and ramp. I craned on tiptoe, trying to catch a first glimpse. After seven months of waiting, the duration these last final minutes seemed an eternity.

Finally the ramp was secured and there he stood in the doorway, a graceful, leggy youngster, pausing to survey his new kingdom. Even though some of the horses in the barn were whinnying, Rickenbacker's eyes met and held mine without being distracted by the commotion. He possessed an incredible calm assuredness for a yearling who had just endured such an arduous journey. Amazingly, no sign of stress, nerves or physical debilitation were evident.

I eagerly traded the driver the signed transport papers for the thick cotton lead rope. For the first time since starting this long journey, I could actually stroke the soft winter coat of the colt who had been the object of my desire for the past seven months.

He gave my shoulder a gentle, inquisitive nudge. "Welcome home, Rickenbacker," I whispered softly near his ear. "You certainly were a long time coming."

Down the Aisle

A light breeze tousled my hair. In that zephyr, I felt the comfort of Dad's hand reaching out from the long distant days of Jambalaya to sprinkle Rickenbacker and me with malfus ralfus dust, his special, magical concoction that had always made me believe that all things were possible.

Confidence swelled in me as I ruffled the colt's thick forelock. Without hesitation, I led him forward toward the open stall waiting next to Dauntless, eager for the bright promise of all that still waited down the aisle.

Down the Aisle

Epilogue

My solo ride on Rickenbacker marked a new chapter down the aisle.

It has been two years since that memorable early morning arrival of Rickenbacker. "Eddie", as we quickly nicknamed him has become a fast favorite of anyone who visits Full Cry Farm. Head curiously stretched out over his Dutch door, he is ever ready to greet visitors with ears pricked and eyes bright. It doesn't even require the promise of a carrot treat to illicit that friendly welcome as he just naturally gravitates toward people.

Each hoof beat of our journey has been a pleasure. Watching his daily development from leggy yearling to muscular adolescent maturity is one of the greatest rewards of my aisle, making it possible for me to savor every first time moment. From those initial tentative steps around the "horse eating" wash rack drain to my *tail of a kite* grip on his halter throughout two weeks of fractious hand walking after minor surgery to the introduction of lunge lines, bits and long lines, my hands have guided him from pasture playground to arena classroom.

It's so fitting that as **Down the Aisle** prepares to head into publication, I soloed on "Eddie" for the first time. Months of careful groundwork built a solid communication system from the touch of a hand to a steadying command. It seemed a natural process for us to evolve from leading to lunging to long lining to finally, ultimately, putting foot to stirrup to settle softly atop his waiting back. How extra special the world appeared to me, looking out through those little brown ears, still pricked happily forward expectant for the next lesson.

As my journey continues *Down the Aisle*, I have enjoyed hearing stories that make the texture of other people's aisles so rich. As a way to give voice to those stories, we have developed **DowntheAisleStories.com**, an interactive website where aisle mates, barn buddies and fellow horse lovers can read and post your own special *Down the Aisle* memories in a variety of forms from short stories to snapshots to special moments.

Down the Aisle

We are also showcasing select stories in our ***Down the Aisle*** monthly column which appears in horse publications around the country. If the column is not already running in your favorite horse magazines, contact the editor and ask them to include ***Down the Aisle***.

I look forward to reading the unique, inspiring moments that have made your journey ***Down the Aisle*** as memorable as mine.

Down the Aisle
Order Page

To order on-line, visit http://DowntheAisleStories.com. We accept all major credit cards through our secure PayPal account. If you prefer to pay by check, please fill out the form below and send it to the address provided.

Quantity	**Price**	**Total**
___ Down the Aisle	$19.95	_____
___ Making Magic	$29.95	_____

Breeding and Birthing a Healthy Foal

Shipping & Handling	($3.00 per book)	_____
Total		_____

Shipping Information:

Name: _____
Ship To Address: _____
City: _____
State/Zip: _____
Home Phone: _____

Autograph my books please ___Yes ___ No thanks
Autograph to: _____

Please make checks payable to:
Down the Aisle Promotions

Mail your order with your check to:
Down the Aisle Promotions
5555 St. Rt. 132
Batavia, OH 45103

Watch our website www.DowntheAisleStories.com for the re-release of **Tic-Tac**, the classic young adult novel also written by Leslie McDonald.

Made in the USA
Lexington, KY
05 April 2016